Whispering to AI:

Prompt Engineering for Pharma Brand Managers

Whispering to AI:

Prompt Engineering for Pharma Brand Managers

Subba Rao Chaganti

PharmaMed Press

An imprint of BSP Books Pvt. Ltd.
4-4-309/316, Giriraj Lane,
Sultan Bazar, Hyderabad - 500 095.

Whispering to AI: Prompt Engineering for Pharma Brand Managers
by Subba Rao Chaganti

Published by

PharmaMed Press™
An imprint of BSP Books Pvt. Ltd.
4-4-309/316, Giriraj Lane, Sultan Bazar, Hyderabad - 500 095.
Phone: 040-23445688, 23445600; Fax: 91+40-23445611
E-mail: info@pharmamedpress.com
www.pharmamedpress.com/pharmamedpress.net

ISBN: 978-93-49562-43-1 (Hardback)

DISCLAIMER

The information in this book, **Whispering to AI: Prompt Engineering for Pharma Brand Managers,** is presented for informational purposes only and should not be construed as medical advice. It is intended for a general audience and does not substitute for the professional judgment of a healthcare provider.

The author and publisher make no warranties, express or implied, concerning the accuracy, completeness, or timeliness of the content within this book. Readers are always advised to consult qualified healthcare professionals regarding health or medical conditions.

Artificial intelligence (AI) and prompt engineering in pharmaceutical marketing are rapidly evolving fields. The author has endeavored to provide current and relevant information at the time of publication. However, readers are encouraged to stay updated on this domain's latest advancements and best practices.

Examples and case studies presented in this book are for illustrative purposes only and may not reflect the specific practices of any particular pharmaceutical company. Finally, mentioning specific products or services within this book does not constitute an endorsement by the author or the publisher.

PREFACE

The world of pharmaceutical marketing stands at the precipice of artificial intelligence (AI). Specifically, prompt engineering offers a powerful tool to craft compelling and impactful brand experiences for patients and healthcare professionals (HCPs). This book, "Whispering to AI: Prompt Engineering for Pharma Brand Managers," is your compass on this exciting journey.

Gone are the days of generic marketing messages. Patients today demand personalized experiences that address their specific needs and concerns. Here, we will explore the transformative potential of prompt engineering, empowering you to create content that resonates deeply with your target audience.

But AI is not a magic bullet. This book emphasizes the crucial role of human creativity. It's about forging a powerful partnership between human ingenuity and AI's effciency. We explore how to leverage AI to personalize patient education, craft data-driven brand strategies, and navigate the ever-evolving ethical considerations in this domain.

Packed with practical examples, industry trends, and future-oriented thinking, this book equips you with the knowledge and strategies to harness the power of prompt engineering in pharma marketing. Whether you are a seasoned marketing professional or just starting your journey in this dynamic field, this guide will illuminate the path toward creating impactful and ethical content that serves patients, builds trust with HCPs, and shapes healthcare.

So, turn the page and embark on this exploration of prompt engineering in pharmaceutical marketing. Let's unlock AI's potential to forge meaningful connections, empower patients, and revolutionize how pharmaceutical brands connect with the world.

Subba Rao Chaganti

ACKNOWLEDGMENTS

Writing a book is rarely a solitary endeavor, and this one, exploring the exciting intersection of AI and pharma branding, is no exception. I am deeply grateful to the many individuals and forces that have shaped this project, from its initial idea to its culmination in these pages.

First and foremost, I must acknowledge the profound impact of the rapidly evolving field of Artificial Intelligence. Advancements in language models and the burgeoning potential of prompt engineering have been constant sources of inspiration and fascination. This book is a testament to the power of these tools and their potential to revolutionize how we approach pharma marketing.

I sincerely thank my publishers, Anil Shah and Nikunjesh Shah, for their belief in this project and guidance. I also thank Naresh Daver and his team for their meticulous attention to detail and support. Their expertise has been instrumental in shaping the final form of this book.

I am also indebted to the numerous thought leaders, researchers, and practitioners in AI, marketing, and pharmaceuticals, whose work has laid the foundation for this book.

I also thank Srinivasa Phanindra for designing a beautiful cover for this book.

This book would not have been possible without the support and encouragement of my family and friends. Their patience, understanding, and unwavering belief in me have been a constant source of strength. To Mahalakshmi Changanti, my life partner in every sense of the word, you were my rock and endless source of encouragement. Thank you for sharing this adventure and being my muse and anchor.

To my children and their spouses— Srinivasa Phanindra and Geetha, Lavanya, Satya Shankara Aditya, Soumya, and Chaitanya Rao—your love and belief in me fueled my spirit. To my grandchildren—Eesha, Aditi, Surya, and Shriya, thank you for being my biggest cheerleaders.

Finally, I want to acknowledge the hypothetical pharmaceutical brand GlucoWell, a practical case study throughout this book. While fictional, GlucoWell represents the many real-world challenges and opportunities faced by pharmaceutical brand managers in today's dynamic landscape. Its journey through the world of prompt engineering will provide readers with valuable insights and practical tools they can apply to their brands.

While I have strived to acknowledge everyone who contributed to this project, any omissions are unintentional. I am deeply grateful to all those who have supported me in big and small ways. I hope this book is a valuable resource for pharmaceutical brand managers navigating the exciting new world of AI-powered marketing.

-Author

CONTENTS

Part I. The Rise of AI and the Prompt Engineering Revolution in Pharma

The pharmaceutical industry is poised for a transformative revolution driven by rapid Artificial Intelligence (AI) advancements. This revolution will reshape how pharmaceutical companies approach drug discovery, clinical trials, marketing, and patient engagement. At the heart of this transformation lies a powerful technique known as prompt engineering.

Prompt engineering involves crafting specific instructions or prompts to guide AI models in generating desired text formats. By leveraging the capabilities of AI, pharma companies can unlock new opportunities, streamline processes, and improve patient outcomes.

This section explores the exciting world of AI and prompt engineering. We delve into how these technologies revolutionize the pharmaceutical industry and discuss their potential benefits. You will learn about the key applications of AI and prompt engineering, from drug discovery to patient education.

Get ready to embark on a journey that will equip you with the knowledge and tools to harness the power of AI and prompt engineering for your pharmaceutical marketing initiatives. The future of pharmaceuticals is here, powered by innovation and technology.

CHAPTER

1

Introduction: The AI Revolution in Pharma Marketing

The pharmaceutical marketing landscape is undergoing a significant transformation. Gone are the days of bombarding healthcare professionals (HCPs) with generic messages and relying on expensive one-size-fits-all campaigns. Today, the industry faces an information overload challenge. Busy HCPs struggle to keep up with the constant influx of emails, conferences, and drug representative visits promoting new medications. Additionally, traditional marketing methods like TV ads and print campaigns are becoming increasingly cost-prohibitive.

This is where Artificial Intelligence (AI) enters the scene, offering a beacon of hope for pharma marketers. AI, particularly through the power of prompt engineering, is revolutionizing pharmaceutical marketing by:

1. **Personalizing the Approach**: Imagine Dr. Williams, a primary care physician inundated with marketing messages. AI can personalize Dr. Williams's experience by analyzing her patient demographics and area of expertise. This allows pharmacists and companies to send her targeted information about medications relevant to her patient population, like a new diabetes treatment, if she sees a rise in Type 2 diabetes cases.
2. **Boosting Efficiency and Insights**: AI automates tedious tasks like content creation and data analysis, freeing up valuable time for pharmaceutical marketing teams to focus on strategic

initiatives. Additionally, AI can analyze vast datasets of patient information and generate valuable insights that inform marketing strategies.

3. **The Powerhouse of AI: Large Language Models (LLMs)**: Think of LLMs as highly skilled chefs with a vast knowledge of culinary recipes (text data). Like a chef needs a specific recipe to create a dish, LLMs require clear instructions (prompts) to perform tasks eûectively.
4. **Prompt Engineering: The Secret Sauce**: Prompt engineering is crafting eûective instructions (prompts) to get the desired output from LLMs. It's like providing the chef with a detailed recipe, specifying ingredients, cooking methods, and desired flavors. In pharma marketing, a prompt engineer might instruct an LLM: "Write a social media post in a friendly and informative tone for patients with Type 2 diabetes, highlighting the benefits of our new medication and its ability to improve blood sugar control."

A Future Fueled by AI

The Potential of AI in pharma marketing extends far beyond the examples provided. Imagine AI-powered chatbots providing 24/7 patient support or analyzing patient sentiment from online reviews to understand brand perception. By embracing AI and the power of prompt engineering, pharma companies can create personalized campaigns that resonate with HCPs and patients, leading to improved healthcare outcomes.

1.1 Why Pharma Needs AI: The Evolving AI Landscape

The world of pharmaceutical marketing is undergoing a significant shift. Traditional methods, once effective, are struggling to keep pace with the ever-changing healthcare landscape. Here's a closer look at the two major challenges pharma marketing faces today:

1. **Information Overload for Healthcare Professionals (HCPs)**:

   Imagine Dr. Rodriguez, a busy cardiologist who manages patient appointments, research, and administrative tasks. Her inbox overflows with emails from various pharmaceutical companies promoting new medications. She also receives flyers and drug representatives' visits, all vying for her attention. This information overload makes it difficult for Dr. Rodriguez to stay current on the latest advancements and identify relevant treatments for her patients.

   Examples of Information Overload:

   - **Multiple Channels**: Pharma companies bombard HCPs with information across various channels: emails, phone calls, conferences, drug representative visits, and online advertisements. This creates a scattered and overwhelming experience.
   - **Generic Messaging**: Marketing materials often lack personalization, promoting medications to all HCPs regardless of the specialty and the patient population. This generic approach wastes Dr. Rodriguez's time and does not address her specific needs.
   - **Unfiltered Content**: The sheer volume of information available makes it challenging for HCPs to identify credible and reliable sources. Dr. Rodriguez may struggle to differentiate valuable clinical trial data from promotional materials.

2. **Rising Costs of Traditional Marketing**:
   - Traditional pharma marketing methods like television commercials, print advertisements, and large-scale conferences are becoming increasingly cost-prohibitive.

   Examples of Rising Costs:
   - **Expensive Media Buys**: Securing prime television advertising slots or preeminent medical journal placements comes at a hefty price.
   - **Limited Reach**: Traditional media may not reach the most relevant audience segments. A TV ad promoting a new diabetes medication might miss targeted populations like young adults or those in rural areas.
   - **Lack of Measurability**: Measuring the return on investment (ROI) from traditional methods can be challenging. Dr. Rodriguez might receive hundreds of drug rep visits, but it isn't easy to track which ones influence her prescribing habits.

The Impact

These challenges significantly impact the effectiveness of pharmaceutical marketing. HCPs struggle to stay informed, and patients may not receive the most relevant treatment options. Additionally, rising costs limit the resources available for the research and development of new medications.

Why Pharma Needs AI: The Evolving Landscape

All these challenges necessitate pharmaceutical companies to increasingly turn to artificial intelligence (AI) to navigate the complex and rapidly evolving healthcare landscape. Here are some important reasons why AI is becoming indispensable for pharma:

1. **Personalized Medicine**:
   - AI can analyze vast patient data to identify patterns and develop personalized treatment plans.

- This enables more effective interventions tailored to individual needs, improving patient outcomes.
- **Example**: A pharma company uses AI to analyze a patient's genetic data and medical history to identify the most effective treatment for their specific type of cancer.

2. **Drug Discovery and Development**:
   - AI can accelerate drug discovery by analyzing molecular data to identify potential drug targets and predict their efficacy. This can significantly reduce the time and cost of bringing new drugs to market.
   - **Example**: A pharmaceutical company uses AI to screen millions of molecules to identify potential new drug candidates, accelerating drug discovery.
3. **Clinical Trials:**
   - AI can optimize clinical trial design and recruitment, leading to more efficient and cost-eûective studies.
   - AI can also quickly analyze patient data from clinical trials to identify trends and adverse events.
   - **Example**: An AI-powered platform efficiently matches patients to clinical trials, reducing recruitment time and improving study outcomes.
4. **Supply Chain Management**:
   - AI can inform and predict pharmaceutical demand, optimize inventory levels, and improve supply chain efficiency.
   - This helps ensure that patients have access to the medications they need when they need them.
   - **Example**: A pharma company uses AI to predict demand for a new medication, ensuring sufficient supply to meet patient needs without excess inventory.
5. **Regulatory Compliance**:
   - AI can help pharma companies comply with complex regulations and ensure data privacy.

- AI-powered systems can monitor for non-compliance and provide early warnings of potential issues.
- **Example**: An AI-powered system monitors regulatory changes and ensures that a pharmaceutical company's products and practices remain compliant.

6. **Patient Engagement and Education**:
   - AI-powered chatbots and virtual assistants can provide personalized patient support and education.
   - This can improve patient adherence to treatment plans and overall health outcomes.
   - **Example**: A pharmaceutical company developing an AI-powered chatbot that can answer patients' questions about their medications and provide personalized support.

7. **Competitive Advantage**:
   - Pharma companies that embrace AI will have a significant competitive advantage.
   - AI can help companies develop innovative new products and services that meet the evolving needs of patients and healthcare providers.
   - **Example**: A pharma company uses AI to develop an AI-powered chatbot that can answer patients' questions about their medications and provide personalized support.

In conclusion, AI is becoming essential for pharmaceutical companies to stay competitive and improve patient outcomes. By leveraging AI, pharmaceutical companies can unlock new opportunities, address challenges, and drive innovation in the healthcare industry.

The Rise of Prompt Engineering in Pharma Marketing

Prompt engineering, a technique for crafting specific instructions for AI models, has emerged as a powerful tool for revolutionizing pharmaceutical marketing.

Pharmaceutical companies can generate highly targeted, personalized, and engaging content by leveraging AI's capabilities.

Key Applications of Prompt Engineering in Pharma:

1. **Personalized Patient Education**: AI-powered chatbots and virtual assistants, guided by carefully crafted prompts, can provide tailored information and support to patients. This helps address specific concerns, improve medication adherence, and enhance the overall patient experience.
2. **Targeted Marketing Campaigns**: Prompt engineering enables the creation of highly targeted marketing campaigns that resonate with specific patient segments.

   By understanding patient demographics, preferences, and online behavior, pharma companies can deliver relevant messages through social media, email, and other channels.
3. **Content Generation and Optimization**: AI models can generate various content formats, such as blog posts, social media posts, and email newsletters. Prompt engineering ensures that this content is aligned with the brand's voice, message, and target audience.
4. **Data-Driven Insights**: Prompt engineering can analyze vast amounts of data to gain insights into patient behavior, market trends, and competitor activities. This information can inform marketing strategies and product development.
5. **Regulatory Compliance**: AI can help pharma companies ensure their marketing materials comply with complex regulations. By using prompts to generate content that adheres to specific guidelines, pharma companies can avoid costly penalties and maintain a positive reputation.

Examples of Successful Applications:

- **Personalized Patient Education**: A pharmaceutical company uses AI to create personalized medication reminders tailored to patients' preferences and schedules.

- **Targeted Marketing Campaigns**: A pharma company develops social media campaigns targeting specific patient segments based on age, location, and health conditions.
- **Content Generation**: A pharma company uses AI to generate an informative blog posts and articles on various topics related to their products and services.

Conclusion

Prompt engineering has the potential to transform the way pharmaceutical companies interact with patients and healthcare professionals. By leveraging the power of AI, pharma companies can create more engaging, relevant, and effective marketing campaigns that drive brand awareness, patient engagement, and improved health outcomes.

1.2. The Power of Language Models: How AI is Changing the Game

Large Language Models (LLMs) are the workhorses behind the AI revolution in pharma marketing. Imagine them as vast digital libraries containing information on a massive scale, but unlike traditional libraries, LLMs can not only access information but also process and generate human-like text. Here's a breakdown of how LLMs, guided by prompt engineering, can be instrumental in pharma marketing:

1. **Enhanced Content Generation and Communication**:
    - Imagine generating high-quality patient education materials, social media posts, or even press releases in a fraction of the time. LLMs can be your secret weapon for crafting informative content:
    - **Example**: A pharma company must create patient information leaflets for their new diabetes medication. A prompt for an LLM could be: "Write a patient information leaflet in a clear and concise style, explaining the benefits, side effects, and dosage instructions for our new diabetes medication. Ensure the information aligns with FDA guidelines and maintains a patient-friendly tone."
    - Leveraging its knowledge base, the LLM can generate a draft leaflet that requires minimal editing from human professionals.
2. **Personalized Patient Education and Support**:
    - Gone are the days of generic brochures. LLMs can create personalized patient education materials tailored to individual needs and literacy levels.
    - **Example**: A patient diagnosed with a rare form of leukemia receives a series of educational emails generated by an LLM. Prompts can guide the LLM in explaining the specific type of leukemia treatment options, including the patient's prescribed medication, and potential side effects, all in a clear and easy-to-understand manner.

This personalized approach empowers patients with relevant information and fosters a better understanding of their condition.

3. **AI-Powered Chatbots for 24/7 Support**:
   - Imagine a virtual assistant readily available to answer basic medication questions and address mild side effects. LLMs can power chatbots that provide patients with immediate support.
   - **Example**: A patient taking a new medication for high blood pressure can use a chatbot to track their medication schedule, receive reminders to take their medication on time, and get answers to frequently asked questions about potential side effects or interactions with other medications.

   The chatbot, guided by prompts outlining appropriate responses and educational materials can alleviate the burden on healthcare professionals by readily addressing basic patient inquiries.

4. **Streamlining Regulatory Processes**:

   The regulatory approval process for new medications is often complex and involves extensive documentation. LLMs can assist in this process by analyzing and summarizing data.

   - **Example**: A pharmaceutical company must compile a comprehensive safety report for its new drug candidate. When prompted with relevant clinical trial data and safety reports, an LLM can analyze the information and generate a concise summary highlighting potential risks and benefits, expediting the regulatory review process.

5. **Language Translation for Global Reach**:

   The pharmaceutical industry operates globally. LLMs can translate marketing materials and patient education resources into multiple languages, ensuring global reach and patient education.

   - **Example**: A pharmaceutical company wants to launch its new cancer treatment in Europe and Asia. LLMs can be instructed to translate the website content, patient education leaflets, and press releases in multiple languages, such as French, Spanish and Mandarin Chinese while maintaining scientific accuracy and clarity of the original information.

Remember:

LLMs are still under development, and their outputs require human oversight and verification, especially in the healthcare domain. However, when used responsibly and guided by well-crafted prompts, LLMs hold immense potential to revolutionize pharma by creating personalized communication channels, streamlining processes, and improving patient care globally.

1.3 Enter Prompt Engineering

The Key to Unlocking AI's Potential in Pharma

Large Language Models (LLMs) are powerful tools, but just like a high-performance engine needs clear instructions to function optimally, LLMs require **prompt engineering** to unlock their true potential in the pharmaceutical industry. Here is how crafting effective prompts is the key to success:

1. **Specificity is Key: Tailoring Prompts for Desired Outputs** Imagine instructing a chef to"make a meal." The results would be unpredictable. Effective, prompt engineering provides **specific instructions** to the LLM.
   - **Generic Prompt:** "Write a blog post about our new cholesterol medication." (This might result in a broad and unfocused piece).
   - **Specific Prompt:** "Write a blog post explaining how our new medication helps manage cholesterol levels for patients with high cholesterol. Include dosage information, potential side effects, and how it compares to existing medications, all in an easy-to-understand and objective tone."

   The prompt guides the LLM in generating a targeted, informative blog post that resonates with the target audience.

2. **Context is King: Providing Background Information**

   Imagine a chef unfamiliar with Italian cuisine attempting to make pasta. Providing context is crucial. Similarly, prompts need to contextualize the task for the LLM.
   - **Prompt:** "Our company develops innovative diabetes medications. We are launching a new drug with a novel mechanism of action. Write a press release announcing this launch."

   This prompt provides context about the company, the medication, and the target audience (healthcare professionals) for the LLM to generate a relevant and impactful press release.

3. **Control the Tone and Style: Guiding the LLM's Voice**

   Imagine a chef who can whip up a fancy French dish but needs help with casual food. Prompt engineering allows you to control the LLM's "voice."

   - **Prompt**: "Write a social media post in a friendly and informative tone, promoting our new allergy medication to young adults. Highlight its effectiveness and ease of use while maintaining a professional and trustworthy voice."

   The prompt specifies the desired tone (friendly, informative) and target audience (young adults) to ensure the LLM generates a social media post that resonates with them.

4. **Harnessing Examples for Improved Accuracy**

   Imagine showing a chef a picture of the desired dish for inspiration. Similarly, prompts can be enhanced by including **examples**.

   - **Prompt:** "Write a series of email newsletters for patients taking our new cholesterol medication. The tone should be informative and encouraging for reference, and you can find examples of successful patient education emails from our competitor X."

   The LLM can understand the desired format and style by including relevant examples, leading to more accurate and eûective communication.

5. **Utilizing Keywords for Targeted Results**

   Imagine searching for a recipe online and including keywords like "vegetarian" or "low-carb." Similarly, including **keywords** in prompts allows for targeted content generation.

   - **Prompt**: "Develop a series of web banners promoting our new migraine medication. Target the banners to users experiencing frequent migraines. Include keywords like 'migraine-relief,' 'fast-acting,' and 'clinically proven' in the banner copy."

   These keywords will guide the LLM to generate web banners specifically focused on reaching the target audience experiencing migraines and highlighting the medication's key benefits.

Pharma companies can unlock AI's true potential by mastering these steps in prompt engineering. Tailored prompts ensure the LLM generates content that resonates with the target audience, delivers valuable information, and improves patient care.

CHAPTER

2

Demystifying Prompt Engineering

Prompt engineering is a specialized field within artificial intelligence (AI) that involves crafting specific instructions or prompts to guide large language models (LLMs) in generating desired text formats. It's a crucial skill for leveraging the full potential of AI for various applications, including content creation, translation, and summarization.

Key Characteristics of Prompt Engineering:

- **Task-oriented**: Prompts are designed to achieve specific goals, such as writing a poem, translating a text, or summarizing a document.
- **Human-Machine Interaction**: Prompt engineering involves understanding how to communicate with AI models through natural language prompts effectively.
- **Iterative Process**: Creating effective prompts often involves a process of trial and error, where prompts are refined and adjusted based on the generated outputs.
- **Contextual Understanding**: Prompts should be tailored to the specific context and domain of the desired output.

Examples of Prompt Engineering Tasks:

- **Content Creation**: Generating articles, blog posts, social media content, or product descriptions.

- **Translation**: Translating text from one language to another.
- **Summarization**: Creating concise summaries of longer texts or documents.
- **Creative Writing**: Generating poems, stories, or scripts.
- **Question Answering**: Answering questions based on provided information.

Identifying Prompt Engineering in Practice:

- **Observe the Use of Natural Language**: If AI models are used to process or generate human-readable text, prompt engineering is likely involved.
- **Look for Tailored Instructions**: These are specific instructions or questions given to the AI model to guide its output.
- **Notice the Iterative Process**: Prompt engineering is used if the AI model's outputs are refined or adjusted based on feedback.

Identifying prompt engineering involves recognizing the use of natural language instructions to guide AI models in producing desired text formats. This skill is crucial for anyone working with large language models and AI-powered content creation tools.

Prompt engineering is a rapidly evolving field that has recently gained significant attention. As large language models (LLMs) become increasingly sophisticated, the ability to craft effective prompts has become essential for harnessing their full potential. This chapter aims to demystify prompt engineering and provide a solid foundation for understanding its applications and techniques.

In the following sections, we will explore:

- **What is prompt engineering?** A clear definition and explanation of its role in AI.
- **Key components of a well-crafted prompt**: The essential elements to consider when designing effective prompts.
- **Common pitfalls and best practices**: Tips for avoiding mistakes and achieving optimal results.

By the end of this chapter, you will have a solid grasp of the fundamentals of prompt engineering and be well-prepared to delve deeper into its applications and techniques in the subsequent chapters.

2.1 What is Prompt Engineering?

The Secret Weapon for Unlocking AI's Power in Pharma

Imagine you have a powerful microscope capable of revealing intricate details but need precise instructions to focus it on the specific cells you want to examine. This is analogous to the role of prompt engineering in the world of AI-powered pharma marketing. Large Language Models (LLMs) hold immense potential, but we must guide them with effective prompts to unlock their true value. Here are the details:

What is Prompt Engineering?

Prompt engineering is the art of crafting clear and concise instructions that tell an LLM what information to generate and how to present it. Think of it as writing a detailed recipe for the LLM, your AI chef, to follow in creating your desired content.

Why is it Important in Pharma?

The pharmaceutical industry relies on accurate and targeted communication.

Traditional marketing methods often struggle with this. Prompt engineering empowers you to:

- **Personalize Communication**: Craft prompts to generate content tailored to different healthcare professionals (HCPs) or patient groups. For example, imagine generating separate sets of materials for cardiologists about a new heart medication while creating patient-friendly explainer videos for those taking the medication.
- **Boost Efficiency**: Automate repetitive tasks like content creation. Imagine generating social media posts or patient education materials in a fraction of the time compared to traditional methods.
- **Increase Accuracy**: Guide the LLM to access and process relevant information.

Imagine prompting an LLM to analyze clinical trial data and generate a concise report highlighting key findings for regulatory agencies.

Core Principles of Effective Prompt Engineering:

Here is your toolkit for crafting powerful prompts:

1. **Specificity is Key**: Avoid ambiguity. Instead of saying, "Write about our new drug," specify the target audience (e.g., patients, HCPs), desired content type (e.g., blog post, social media caption), and key information to be included.
2. **Content is King**: Provide background information about your company, the medication, and the target audience. This helps the LLM understand the prompt's purpose and generate relevant content.
3. **Tone and Style**: Do you want a formal press release or a patient-friendly explainer video? Indicate the desired voice in your prompt to ensure the LLM generates content that aligns with your goals.
4. **Leveraging Examples**: Include examples of successful content or competitor materials to guide the LLM toward the desired outcome.
5. **Harnessing Keywords**: Target your audience effectively by incorporating relevant keywords associated with the medication of the disease state.

Examples in Action:

Let's see how prompt engineering translates into practical applications:

Example #1:

- **Scenario**: Develop a series of social media posts promoting a new allergy medicaiton.
- **Prompt**: "Write a series of engaging social media posts for patients aged 18 to 35, promoting our new allergy medication. Highlight its effectiveness in alleviating symptoms and its convenient once-a-day dosage. Maintain a friendly and

informative tone, using keywords like 'allergy relief,' 'fast-acting,' and 'non-drowsy.'

Example #2:

- **Scenario**: Generate a patient information leaflet for a new medication for high blood pressure.
- **Prompt**: "Write a patient information leaflet in a clear and concise style, explaining the benefits and potential side effects of our new medication for high blood pressure. Include information on dosage instructions, potential interactions with other medications, and how to manage side effects, ensure the information aligns with FDA guidelines and maintains a patient-friendly tone."

The Takeaway: Prompt engineering is the key to unlocking AI's potential in pharmaceutical marketing. Mastering this art enables you to craft effective prompts that generate targeted, informative, and engaging content. This will ultimately improve communication with HCPs and patients and improve healthcare outcomes.

2.2 The Anatomy of a Perfect Prompt Instruction: Context and Control

AI-powered Large Language Models (LLMs) are emerging as game-changers in the ever-evolving pharma marketing world. However, like a high-performance engine that needs precise instructions to function optimally, LLMs require well-crafted prompts to unleash their true potential. Here is an exploration into the anatomy of perfect prompt instruction, focusing on context and control:

1. **Building Context: The Foundation of a Powerful Prompt**:
    - Imagine a chef unfamiliar with a specific cuisine attempting to prepare a dish. The results would likely be disappointing. Similarly, a prompt lacking context leaves the LLM is in the dark about the task. Here is how to establish a strong contextual foundation:
    - **Company and Product Background**: Briefly introduce your company's expertise and the provided medication or service.
    - **Target Audience**: Clearly define who you're trying to reach, whether it's cardiologists for a new heart medication or patients with a specific disease.
    - **Communication Goals**: Specify the desired outcome to educate patients, raise awareness among HCPs or generate leads.

    Example: "Our company, a leader in innovative diabetes treatments, is launching 'GlucoWell,' a new medication for Type 2 diabetes management. We aim to develop a series of patient education emails targeting individuals diagnosed with Type 2 diabetes."
2. **Taking Control: Guiding the LLM's Output**:

    Imagine a musician receiving sheet music with just the notes but lacking instructions on tempo, dynamics, or mood. The resulting performance might be technically accurate but devoid of emotion or impact. Similarly, prompts need to guide the LLM's output in terms of:

- **Content-Type**: Specify the format of the desired content — a blog post, social media caption, press release, or patient information leaflet.
- **Desired Tone and Style**: Indicate the voice you want the LLM to adopt —informative and friendly for patient education or formal and authoritative for a press release.
- **Key Information and Keywords**: Outline the crucial details that must be included and relevant keywords to target the specific audience and disease state.

Example: "...The emails should be informative and encouraging, focusing on how GlucoWell helps manage blood sugar levels. Include information on dosage, potential side effects, and tips for medication adherence. Use keywords like "Type 2 diabetes," "blood sugar control," and "lifestyle modifications."

3. **The Art of Specificity: Tailoring the Prompt for Optimal Results**:

   The key to unlocking the true power of prompt engineering lies in **specificity**. Avoid generic instructions. Instead, provide a clear roadmap for the LLMs to follow:

   - **Clearly Defined Tasks**: Instead of saying, "Write about diabetes," specify the desired action — 'Explain the risk factors for developing Type 2 diabetes."
   - **Structured Approach**: Break down complex tasks into smaller, more manageable steps for the LLM.
   - **Desired Length and Format**: Indicate the generated content's preferred word count or structure (e.g., bullet points, numbered list).

Example (Continuation):

"...Each email should be approximately 300 words long and structured as follows:

Introduction - briefly explain Type 2 diabetes and its management. Benefits of GlucoWell - highlight the key advantages of medicaiton. Dosage and Side effects -provide clear instructions and potential side effects. Medication Adherence Tips - offer strategies for taking GlucoWell consistently."

Conclusion: The Power of Context and Control

By focusing on context and control in your prompt engineering, you equip yourself with the necessary information to generate accurate, targeted, engaging content that aligns with your goals. This empowers you to create a powerful communication strategy in the dynamic world of pharmaceutical marketing, fostering better patient education, and improved health outcomes.

2.3 Different Prompt Engineering Techniques: From Simple to Advanced (including Chain Prompting)

The world of prompt engineering for AI-powered pharma marketing offers a diverse toolkit. Let's explore various techniques, progressing from simple to advanced, showcasing how they can be used to generate effective content:

1. **Simple Prompts: Setting the Foundation**

   These prompts provide basic instructions for the LLM, ideal for tasks requiring straightforward outputs:

   - **Example**: "Write a blog post about the benefits of our new cholesterol medication."

     This straightforward prompt will generate a little highlighting of the medication's advantages.

2. **Informative Prompts: Adding Context and Clarity**

   These prompts offer additional information, improving LLM's understanding of the desired content:

   - **Example**: "Our company specializes in developing innovative cardiovascular medications. Write a blog post targeting patients with high cholesterol, highlighting the benefits of our new medication, 'CholesterolEase."This prompt provides context about the company, target audience, and medication name, making the post more informative.

3. **Instructional Prompts: Guiding the LLM's Style**

   These prompts specify the desired tone and style of the output:

   - **Example**: "Write a blog post for patients with high cholesterol in a friendly and informative tone, emphasizing how 'CholesterolEase' can help them manage their cholesterol levels effectively."

   This prompt specifies the target audience, tone, and desired outcome, leading to a post that resonates with patients.

4. **Keyword-Rich Prompts: Targeting the Right Audience**

   These prompts incorporate relevant keywords to ensure the generated content reaches the intended audience:

   - **Example**: "Write a blog post title targeting patients searching online for 'high cholesterol treatment.' Include keywords like 'CholesterolEase,' 'lower cholesterol,' and 'healthy heart.'

   This prompt uses keywords likely used by patients seeking information, resulting in a title that appears in relevant search results.

5. **Example-Based Prompts: Demonstrating the Desired Outcome**

   These prompts offer examples of similar content to guide the LLM:

   - **Example**: "Write a blog post title for patients with high cholesterol, similar to "10 Tips to Manage Cholesterol Levels Effectively,' highlighting the benefits of 'CholesterolEase." Providing an existing title structure helps the LLM generate a similar format while focusing on the specific medication.

6. **Chain Prompting: Building Upon Previous Outputs**

   This advanced technique involves creating a series of prompts that build upon each other, allowing for complex content generation:

   - **Example 1 (Initial Prompt)**: "Write a blog introduction explaining high cholesterol and its risks."
   - **Example 2 (Chain Prompt)**: "Based on the previous introduction, write a section explaining how "CholesterolEase' can help manage cholesterol levels and reduce these health risks."

   Chain prompting allows for longer, more comprehensive content, like a blog post with multiple sections.

Conclusion: Choosing the Right Tool for the Job

Prompt engineering offers a spectrum of techniques for pharmaceutical marketers. The right approach depends on the task's complexity and desired outcome. Mastering simple prompts lays the groundwork, while advanced techniques like chain prompting unlock the potential for generating intricate and informative content. By understanding and utilizing these techniques, pharmaceutical companies can harness the power of AI to create targeted, engaging, and informative content, promoting better patient understanding and healthcare outcomes.

2.4 Case Studies: How Pharma Companies are Using Prompt Engineering Today

The world of pharmaceutical marketing is embracing the power of prompt engineering. Here are a few compelling case studies showcasing how leading companies are leveraging this technology:

Case Study #1: Personalizing Patient Education with Empathy

Company: Renowned Diabetes Treatment Provider, "Diabetic Solutions Inc."

Challenge: Diabetic Solutions noticed a decline in patient engagement with their one-size-fits-all email newsletters. Patients reported the materials felt impersonal and lacked a connection to their specific needs and challenges.

Solution: Diabetic Solutions implemented prompt engineering to personalize email content based on patient data:

- **Data Integration**: They integrated their patient database with the LLM, allowing prompts to access information like:
- Age group (tailoring language complexity)
- Duration of diagnosis (focusing on newly diagnosed vs. long-term management). Specific medications prescribed (providing targeted information on complementary therapies)
- **Empathy Prompts**: Prompts were crafted to encourage the LLM to utilize an empathetic and supportive tone, fostering a sense of connection with patients.

Examples:

- "Start the email with a warm greeting, acknowledging the challenges of managing diabetes."
- "Use phrases like 'We understand' and 'You're not alone' to build trust and rapport."

Results: Diabetic Solutions observed a significant increase in patient engagement:

- **Open Rates**: Email open rates doubled compared to generic newsletters.
- **Click-Through Rates**: Click-Through rates on links to educational resources tripled.

- **Patient Feedback**: Surveys revealed that patients felt the emails were more relevant and addressed their specific concerns.

This case highlights the power of using prompt engineering to personalize patient education, leading to better health outcomes.

Case Study #2: Generating High-Quality Content at Scale—A Broader View

Company: Emerging oncology drug developer, "NovaCure Pharmaceuticals."

Challenge: NovaCure, a smaller company, lacked the resources to create a comprehensive marketing campaign for its breakthrough cancer treatment. Traditional methods, like hiring a content creation agency, were cost-prohibitive.

Solution: NovaCure utilized prompt engineering to automate content generation for various platforms:

- **Blog Posts**: Prompts specified target audiences and content goals:
- **Patients**: Prompts focused on explaining the type of cancer, the drug targets, treatment benefits, and potential side effects.
- **Caregivers**: Prompts aimed at providing information on supporting patients undergoing the treatment and potential lifestyle adjustments.
- **HCPs**: Prompts emphasized the drug's mechanism of action, clinical trial data, and dosage recommendations.
- **Social Media Posts**: Prompts outlined engaging formats and key messages:
- **Infographics**: Prompts instructed the LLM to create visually appealing infographics highlighting treatment advantages.
- **Short Videos**: Prompts focused on generating short, informative videos featuring patient testimonials or explainer animations about the drug's function.
- **Press Releases**: Prompts ensured clear and concise communication of the drug launch, targeting relevant scientific journals and news outlets.

Results: Prompt engineering allowed NovaCure to generate a vast amount of high-quality content at a significantly lower cost:

- **Content Diversity**: They were able to create content for various platforms, reaching a wider audience.
- **Faster Time to Market**: Content creation time was drastically reduced, allowing for a quicker marketing campaign launch.
- **Increased Brand Awareness**: The diverse content generated significant interest in NovaCure's new cancer treatment.

This case demonstrates how prompt engineering empowers smaller companies to compete by creating high-quality content efficiently.

Case Study #3: GlobalPharm Leveraged Prompt Engineering to Develop an AI-powered System for Analyzing Customer Feedback

- **Prompt Design**: The prompts instructed the LLM to analyze vast textual data and identify key themes.
- **Sentiment Analysis**: Prompts guided the LLM to categorize feedback as positive, negative, or neutral.
- **Topic Extraction**: Prompts instructed the LLM to identify recurring themes like medication side effects, product efficacy, or customer service experiences.
- **Actionable Insights**: Based on the analysis, the LLM-generated reports highlighting areas requiring improvement:
  - **Product Development**: Identifying frequently mentioned side eûects could inform product reformulation or the development of complementary medications.
  - **Marketing Strategies**: Understanding patient concerns about efficacy could guide content creation strategies to address those concerns.
  - **Patient Support Services**: Recognizing negative experiences with customer service could prompt improvements in training or communication channels.

Results: GlobalPharma observed significant improvements after implementing the AI-powered feedback analysis system:

- **Faster Response Times**: They identified and addressed customer concerns faster, improving customer satisfaction.
- **Data-Driven Decisions**: By understanding patient needs and concerns, GlobalPharm could focus on developing products that better address them.

Future Implications:

This case study highlights the potential of prompt engineering for:

- **Predictive Analytics**: LLMs could analyze customer feedback to predict future trends and identify potential product issues before they arise.

- **Building Patient Relationships**: Companies can strengthen patient relationships by leveraging feedback to address concerns and improve products/services.

Conclusion

These case studies illustrate the immense potential of prompt engineering. Prompt engineering empowers pharmaceutical companies to personalize patient education, generate high-quality content efficiently, and gain valuable insights from customer feedback. As AI technology continues to evolve, prompt engineering offers exciting possibilities for the future of pharmaceutical marketing, leading to better communication, improved patient experiences, and potentially groundbreaking advancements in healthcare.

Part II. Mastering the Art of Prompt Engineering for Pharma Branding

In the dynamic world of pharmaceutical marketing, crafting a strong brand identity is crucial for success. Large Language Models (LLMs) are revolutionizing the game. Still, just like a sculptor needs precise instructions to shape a masterpiece, we need effective prompts to unlock the LLM's potential for pharmaceutical branding. This part explores the art of prompt engineering specifically for building a powerful pharmaceutical brand.

1. **Building Brand Awareness with Targeted Prompts**

   Imagine launching a new medication for a specific condition. You aim to generate content that sparks initial interest and position your brand as a leader. Here is how prompts can help:

   - **Target Audience**: Define who you want to reach, such as healthcare practitioners (HCPs), patients or caregivers.
   - **Brand Message**: Outline the core values and message you want to convey (e.g., innovation, patient-centricity, clinical excellence).
   - **Content-Type**: Specify the desired format — social media posts, blog articles, or press releases.

   Example Prompt:

   "Our company, Thrive Therapeutics, is launching a revolutionary new treatment for chronic pain management. We aim to generate engaging social media posts targeting patients experiencing chronic pain. Highlight our medication's innovative mechanism of action and its potential to improve quality of life. Maintain a hopeful and informative tone, emphasizing our commitment to patient well-being, aligning with our brand message of "Thrive with Comfort."

   This prompt sets the stage for the LLM to generate social media posts that stimulate patient interest, introduce the brand and position it as a solution-oriented leader in chronic pain management.

2. **Cultivating Brand Voice and Identity**

   Imagine a company known for its lighthearted and relatable communication style.

   Prompt engineering allows you to ensure the LLM reflects the brand voice:

   - **Brand Voice Guidelines**: Provide the LLM with your brand voice guidelines – formal, informal, humorous, or authoritative.
   - **Emotional Tone**: Specify the desired emotional connection (e.g., trust, empathy, hope).
   - **Keywords and Examples**: Include keywords associated with your brand values and examples of existing content that reflects your brand voice.

   Example Prompt (Continuaiton):

   "...The social media posts should adopt a friendly and encouraging tone, similar to our existing content on managing chronic pain through lifestyle changes. Use humor where appropriate, and focus on empowering patients to take control of their pain management journey. Include keywords like 'chronic pain relief,' 'improved quality of life,' and 'Thrive Therapeutics – Your Partner in Comfort."

   This continuation strengthens the prompt by providing specific guidance on the desired brand voice and emotional connection. This ensures the LLM generates content that resonates with the target audience and reinforces the brand identity.

3. **Leveraging Storytelling for Brand Impact**

   Stories have the power to connect with audiences on a deeper level. Prompts can be used to craft compelling brand narratives:

   - **Brand Story**: Briefly outline your company's history, mission, and values.
   - **Target Audience Needs:** Specify the challenges faced by your target audience.

- **Brand Solution**: Highlight how your product or service addresses those challenges.

Example Prompt:

"Thrive Therapeutics was founded by a team of passionate scientists dedicated to alleviating chronic pain. We believe everyone deserves to live a life free from pain. Write a blog post targeting patients with chronic pain, telling the story of a patient who has found significant relief through our new medicaiton. Emphasize how our medicaiton allows patients to regain control of their lives and pursue their passions."

This prompt empowers the LLM to create a relatable story that showcases your brand's human impact and commitment to patient well-being.

Conclusion: Prompt Engineering—The Key to Powerful Pharma Branding

By mastering the art of prompt engineering, you equip the LLM with the tools to generate content that sparks brand awareness, cultivates a strong brand voice, and leverages storytelling to build emotional connections with your target audience. This ultimately leads to a powerful pharma brand that resonates with patients, HCPs, and stakeholders, paving the way for long-term success. Remember, the possibilities are endless. As AI technology evolves, so will the potential for using prompt engineering to create innovative and impactful branding strategies in the ever-evolving pharma marketing world.

CHAPTER
3

Case Study: Introducing Our Hypothetical Diabetes Medication Brand

Introducing GlucoWell: A New Dawn in Diabetes Management

Imagine a world where managing diabetes feels like a constant struggle and more like a journey towards a healthier, more balanced you. That's the vision behind GlucoWell, a revolutionary diabetes medication poised to disrupt the market.

GlucoWell is more than just a medication; it's a brand built around empowerment and achieving glycemic balance. It targets patients diagnosed with Type 2 diabetes who are looking for a more effective and convenient way to manage their condition.

The Challenge: Correcting the Disbalance in Brand Awareness

GlucoWell, despite its groundbreaking potential, faces a significant challenge — low brand awareness. Several established competitors dominate the market, making it diffcult for GlucoWell to stand out.

The Prompt Engineering Solution: A Multi-Faceted Approach

GlucoWell recognizes the power of prompt engineering and seeks to leverage it to achieve the following goals:

- **Boost Brand Awareness**: Generate content that sparks initial interest and educates patients about GlucoWell's unique benefits.

- **Cultivate Brand Identity**: Craft content that establishes GlucoWell's brand voice, highlighting its core values of empowerment and achieving balance.
- **Targeted Communication**: Develop patient education materials and social media content specifically tailored to the needs and challenges of Type 2 Diabetes.

The following sections will investigate how GlucoWell will utilize prompt engineering for these objectives.

3.1 Brand Identity: Understanding GlucoWell's Core Values and Messaging

Understanding GlucoWell's Core Values and Messaging

GlucoWell's mission to empower patients with Type 2 diabetes and achieve glycemic index balance translates into core values defining its brand identity. These values should resonate with the target audience and guide all communication strategies, including prompt engineering. Here are the GlucoWell's potential core values:

- **Empowerment**: GlucoWell believes in equipping patients with the knowledge and tools to take control of their diabetes management.
- **Balance**: The focus is on achieving a healthy balance between blood sugar levels, lifestyle, and overall well-being.
- **Innovation**: GlucoWell prioritizes the continuous development of effective and convenient solutions for diabetes management.
- **Compassion**: The brand recognizes the challenges people with diabetes face and strives to offer understanding and support.
- **Partnership**: GlucoWell is a partner on the patient's journey toward a healthier life.

Crafting GlucoWell's Brand Messaging

Once the core values are established, GlucoWell can develop key messages that effectively communicate these values to the target audience. These messages should be clear, concise, and emotionally resonant. Here are some potential brand messages for GlucoWell:

- "Take control of your diabetes with GlucoWell" (Empowerment)
- "Achieve glycemic balance and live a healthier life." (Balance)
- "GlucoWell: Innovation for effective diabetes management." (Innovation)

- "We understand the challenges of diabetes. GlucoWell is here to support you." (Compassion and Partnership)
- Partner with GlucoWell on your journey to a healthier you." (Partnership)

Remember, these are just examples, and the ideal core values and messaging will depend on GlucoWell's specific target audience and market positioning.

By incorporating these core values and brand messages into prompts, GlucoWell can ensure that all generated content reflects a consistent and compelling brand identity that resonates with patients. The next section will delve into how prompt engineering can be used to achieve GlucoWell's specific goals.

3.2 Target Audience: Who Are We Trying to Reach with GlucoWell?

Who is GlucoWell Trying to Reach? Understanding Your Target Audience

GlucoWell's success hinges on effectively reaching its target audience – patients diagnosed with Type 2 diabetes. But within this broad category, there may be further segmentation based on factors like:

- **Age**: younger adults (18-45) vs. middle-aged or older adults (46+) might have different needs and communication preferences.
- **Tech-savvy**: Some patients may be comfortable using digital tools for diabetes management, while others might prefer traditional methods.
- **Disease Stage**: Patients newly diagnosed will have different priorities compared to those managing diabetes for many years.
- **Lifestyle**: Activity levels, dietary habits, and overall health status can influence communication strategies.

Understanding Your Audience's Needs and Challenges

By considering these factors, GlucoWell can gain a deeper understanding of its target audience's needs and challenges:

- Frustration with managing blood sugar levels.
- Feeling overwhelmed by the amount of information available.
- Difficulty maintaining a healthy diet and exercise routine. Lack of motivation and support.
- Fear of complications associated with diabetes

Tailoring Communication for Impact

Once you understand your audience's needs and challenges, you can tailor your communication strategy, including prompt engineering, to resonate with them. Here are some examples:

- **For younger adults**: Develop social media content with a relatable and informative tone, highlighting how GlucoWell can fit seamlessly into their lives.
- **For tech-savvy patients**: Create interactive tools and educational resources that leverage digital platforms.
- **For newly diagnosed patients,** generate content that clearly explains Type 2 diabetes and emphasizes the benefits of early intervention with GlucoWell.
- **For patients struggling with lifestyle changes**: Offer motivational messages, healthy recipe suggestions, and tips for incorporating exercise into daily routines.
- **For patients concerned about complications**, provide informative content about how GlucoWell can help prevent them and ensure long-term well-being.

GlucoWell can strengthen its connections with patients and establish itself as a trusted partner in their diabetes management journey by using prompt engineering to create targeted content that addresses each audience segment's needs and challenges.

CHAPTER

4

Prompt Engineering for Brand Messaging and Communication

Now that we understand GlucoWell's core values, brand messaging, and target audience, let's explore how prompt engineering can be harnessed to achieve the brand's goals:

1. **Boosting Brand Awareness: Sparking Patient Interest**
    - **Goal**: Generate content that educates patients about GlucoWell and its unique benefits.
    - **Prompt Example**:

      "Write a series of social media posts targeting patients with Type 2 diabetes. Briefly explain how traditional diabetes management can be challenging and introduce GlucoWell as a revolutionary new medication that empowers patients to achieve glycemic balance. Use an encouraging tone and highlight keywords like 'Type 2 diabetes,' 'blood sugar control,' 'empowerment,' and GlucoWell."

    This prompt encourages the LLM to create content that sparks initial interest by acknowledging existing challenges and positioning GlucoWell as a solution.

2. **Cultivating Brand Identity: Crafting a Consistent Voice**
    - **Goal**: Create patient education materials that reflect GlucoWell's core values (empowerment, balance, etc.).

- **Prompt Example**:

  "Develop a comprehensive patient information leaflet for GlucoWell. Maintain a clear and informative tone, emphasizing how GlucoWell helps patients take control of their diabetes management and achieve a healthier lifestyle. Include information on dosage, potential side effects, and tips for integrating GlucoWell into daily routines. Ensure the language aligns with GlucoWell's core values of empowerment and achieving balance."

  This prompt specifies the desired tone, content focus, and alignment with core values, ensuring consistency in brand identity.

3. **Targeted Communication: Tailoring Content for Different Segments**

   - **Goal**: Develop engaging content that resonates with specific audience segments within the Type 2 diabetes demographic.
   - **Prompt Example (For Younger Adults)**:

     "Create a series of short video testimonials for GlucoWell featuring young adults with Type 2 diabetes who share their experiences and how GlucoWell has helped them manage their condition. Maintain a relatable and inspiring tone, showcasing how GlucoWell integrates seamlessly into their active lifestyles. Use humor where appropriate and target platforms like Instagram and TikTok."

     This prompt tailors the content format and tone to resonate with a specific audience segment of younger adults.

Additional Considerations:

- **Brand Voice Guidelines**: Provide the LLM with clear guidelines on GlucoWell's desired brand voice (e.g., friendly, informative, authoritative).

- **Keywords and Examples**: Include relevant keywords associated with GlucoWell's brand messaging and examples of existing content that reflects the desired tone and style.
- **Emotional Connection**: Strive for prompts that evoke positive emotions and build trust with the target audience.

The Power of Prompt Engineering

By crafting effective prompts that incorporate these elements, GlucoWell can leverage the power of AI to generate a variety of content, including:

- Social media posts that raise brand awareness.
- Patient educational materials that inform and empower.
- Blog articles and website content that establish GlucoWell as a thought leader in diabetes management.

Pharma Brand Messaging and Content Generation Using Prompt Engineering if

Some Examples:

1. **Generating Social Media Posts**:
   - **Target Audience:** Patients with allergies
   - **Goal**: Raise awareness about a new allergy medication and its benefits.

   Prompt:

   "Create a series of social media posts for Facebook and Instagram targeting adults suffering from allergies. Use a lighthearted and informative tone, explaining the common struggles of allergies and highlighting how (Brand name) medication effectively relieves symptoms like sneezing, itchy eyes, and runny nose. Incorporate visuals like infographics or short animations to enhance audience engagement.

   Maintain a consistent brand voice that is friendly, approachable, and trustworthy."

2. **Developing Patient Education Materials**:
   - **Target Audience**: Caregivers of patients with Alzheimer's disease.
   - **Goal**: Provide clear and informative resources on managing Alzhelmer's symptoms.

   Prompt:

   "Develop a comprehensive patient education booklet for caregivers of patients diagnosed with Alzheimer's disease. Maintain a compassionate and supportive tone, acknowledging the challenges faced by caregivers. Provide clear information on managing symptoms like memory loss, confusion, and behavioral changes. Include practical tips and resources for daily care activities, medication management, and the emotional well-being of both patients and caregivers. Ensure the language is easy to understand and avoids overly technical terms."

3. **Crafting Blog Posts for Healthcare Professionals (HCPs)**:
   - **Target Audience**: Doctors specializing in oncology.
   - **Goal**: Educate HCPs about the clinical trial results for a new cancer treatment.

   Prompt:

   "Write a concise and informative blog post summarizing the recent successful clinical trial results for (Brand Name), a new medication for treating (Type of Cancer). Focus on key data points like efficacy, safety profile, and patient response rates. Maintain a formal and objective tone, adhering to scientific writing principles. Clearly outline the potential benefits of (Brand Name) for cancer treatment and its implications for clinical practice. Target this blog post for publication in reputable medical journals and HCP online communities."

4. **Generating Press Releases**:
   - **Goal**: Announce the launch of a new medical device.

Prompt:

"Draft a press release announcing the official launch of (Device Name), a revolutionary new medical device designed for (Purpose). Emphasize the innovative technology behind the device and its potential to improve patient outcomes. Highlight key features and benefits compared to existing solutions. Target this press release for distribution to major healthcare publications and media outlets. Maintain a clear, concise, and newsworthy tone throughout the press release."

5. **Creating Compelling Brand Taglines**:
   - **Brand**: Innovative company developing a personalized pain management solution.

   Prompt:

   - Generate a tagline for {Brand Name} that captures the essence of personalized pain management. Focus on keywords like 'personalized approach,' convey a sense of innovation, and resonate with patients suffering from chronic pain."

Conclusion

Prompt engineering is a powerful tool for GlucoWell to achieve its brand communication goals. By understanding the target audience, crafting clear prompts that reflect brand identity, and leveraging the LLMs' capabilities, GlucoWell can generate impactful content that sparks interest, fosters trust, and positions the brand as a leader in empowering patients with Type 2 diabetes to achieve glycemic balance and healthier life.

4.1 Crafting Compelling Brand Taglines and Slogans with Prompts

A well-crafted tagline or slogan can be a powerful brand recognition and memorability tool. Prompt engineering allows you to harness the power of AI to generate creative options that capture your brand essence. Here's how:

1. **Define Your Brand Identity**:
   - Before crafting prompts, take a step back and solidify your brand identity. Consider the following:
   - **Core Values**: What are the fundamental principles that guide your brand?
   - **Target Audience**: Who are you trying to reach? What are their needs and desires?
   - **Brand Differentiation**: What sets you apart from the competition?

2. **Craft Effective Prompts**:

   Once you have a clear understanding of your brand, use prompts to guide the LLM in generating taglines and slogans:
   - **Keyword Focus**: Include relevant keywords that represent your brand and resonate with your target audience.
   - **Emotional Tone**: Specify the desired emotional response you want to evoke (e.g., trust, excitement, empowerment).
   - **Brand Voice**: Indicate whether the tagline should be formal, informal, playful, or authoritative, aligning with your brand voice.

   Examples (Optional): To inspire the generation process, provide the LLM with examples of taglines or slogans you admire, even from other industries.

3. **Refine and Choose the Best Option**:

   The LLM will generate several taglines and slogans based on your prompts. Here is how to refine them:

- **Clarity and Conclusion**: Ensure the tagline is concise and easy to remember.
- **Brand Alignment**: Evaluate if the tagline accurately reflects your brand identity and core values.
- **Target Audience Appeal**: Assess whether the tagline resonates with your target audience and their needs.
- **Testing**: Consider conducting A/B testing to gauge audience preference for different tagline options.

Creating Compelling Taglines and Slogans Using Prompt Engineering— Some Examples:

1. **Breakthrough Medication for Chronic Disease**:
    - **Prompt**: "Generate a tagline for a revolutionary new medication that significantly improves the lives of patients with a chronic disease. Focus on keywords like 'breakthrough treatment,' 'improved quality of life,' and '[Disease Name] management. Maintain a hopeful and empowering tone."
    - **Possible Taglines**:
    - "[Brand Name]; Redefining the future [Disease Name] management."
    - "[Brand Name]: Reclaim your life with effective [Disease Name] control."
    - "[Brand Name]: Hope for a healthier tomorrow with [Disease Name']."
2. **Personalized Cancer Treatment**:
    - **Prompt**: "Develop a tagline for a company offering personalized cancer treatment plans. Emphasize keywords like 'precision medicine,' 'personalized care,' and 'fighting cancer together.'
    - **Possible Taglines**:
    - "[Brand Name] Personalized cancer care, tailored to your unique needs."

- "[Brand Name]: Fighting cancer together, one patient at a time."
- "[Brand Name]: Precision medicine for a more effective fight against cancer."

3. **Mental Health Medication with a Focus on Well-Being**:
   - **Prompt**: "Create a tagline for a medication that effectively treats mental health conditions while emphasizing overall well-being. Include keywords like 'mental health,' well-being journey,' and '[Condition Name] support."
   - **Possible Taglines**:
   - "[Brand Name]: Supporting your mental health journey, one step at a time."
   - "[Brand Name]: Find balance and feel better with [Condition Name] support."
   - "[Brand Name]: "Because Mental well-being matters."

   Remember, these are just examples. The most effective taglines will be unique to your brand and its challenges.

Additional Tips:

- **Consider your target audience**: What are their needs and concerns? Tailor the tagline to resonate with them.
- **Highlight benefits**: Focus on how your medication improves patients' lives.
- **Maintain brand consistency**: Ensure the tagline aligns with your brand voice and messaging.

By experimenting with prompts and remembering these tips, you can leverage prompt engineering to create a tagline that becomes a powerful and memorable representation of your pharma brand.

4.2 Developing Patient Education Materials Using AI

Patient education is crucial in the pharmaceutical industry. AI, specifically prompt engineering, offers exciting possibilities to create informative, engaging, and personalized patient education materials. Here are some examples:

1. **Understanding Patient Needs**:
    - **Challenge:** Traditional patient education materials often lack personalization and may not address diverse patient populations' specific needs and learning styles.
    - **AI Solution**: Prompt engineering allows you to create targeted content by incorporating:
        - **Patient Demographics**: Age, language, technical literacy.
        - **Disease State**: Specific condition and its complexities.
        - **Learning Style**: Visual, auditory, kinesthetic learners.

    Prompt Example:

    "Develop a series of educational videos for patients newly diagnosed with Type 2 diabetes. Target the content for patients aged 40-60 with a moderate level of technical literacy. Incorporate clear visuals and animations to cater to visual learners. Explain core concepts like blood sugar management, medication adherence, and healthy lifestyle choices. Ensure the tone is informative, encouraging, and addresses common concerns of newly diagnosed patients."

2. **Content Variety and Accessibility**:
    - **Challenge:** Traditional materials may be limited in format (written pamphlets) and may not be accessible to patients with disabilities.
    - **AI Solution**: Prompt engineering allows for generating content in various formats:

- **Written Materials**: Pamphlets, articles, Q&A guides.
- **Visuals**: Infographics, animations, short videos.
- **Interactive Elements**: Quizzes, self-assessment tools.

Prompt Example:

"Create a series of interactive modules for a mobile app that educates patients about the benefits and potential side effects of [Medication Name]. Target the content for patients with visual impairments and ensure compatibility with screen reader software.

Utilize clear audio narration and descriptive text to accompany infographics and animations. Include interactive quizzes to enhance knowledge retention and patient engagement."

3. **Cultural Sensitivity and Language Barriers**:
   - **Challenge**: Traditional materials may not be culturally sensitive or translated into languages spoken by diverse patient populations.
   - **AI Solution**: Prompt engineering can help by:
     - **Specifying Target Languages**: Generate materials in multiple languages.
     - **Incorporating Cultural Nuances**: Adapt content to resonate with different cultural backgrounds.

Prompt Example:

"Develop a patient information booklet on medication adherence, translated into Spanish and Mandarin for a diverse patient population. Ensure the language is clear, concise, and culturally sensitive. Incorporate visuals that resonate with the specific cultural contexts of each target audience."

Benefits of Using AI for Patient Education

- **Increased Patient Engagement**: Variety in format and interactivity keeps patients engaged with the learning process.

- **Improved Comprehension**: Tailored content based on learning styles and needs leads to better understanding.
- **Accessibility and Inclusivity**: Catering to diverse patients with disabilities and language barriers promotes inclusivity.
- **Cost-Effectiveness**: AI can streamline content creation and translation processes.
- **Scalability**: Easily generate materials for various patient populations and languages.

AI is not a replacement for human expertise in healthcare communication. However, prompt engineering offers a powerful tool to complement existing practices and create patient education materials that are informative, engaging, and accessible to a wider aucience.

4.3 Building Engaging Social Media Content with Prompts

Social media offers a unique platform for pharma companies to connect with patients, raise awareness about health conditions, and promote their brands. However, creating engaging content in such a dynamic space can be challenging. Prompt engineering can be a game-changer, allowing you to craft content that resonates with your target audience:

1. **Humanizing Pharma with Relatable Stories**:
   - **Challenge**: Pharmaceutical companies are often perceived as impersonal entities.
   - **Solution**: Use prompts to create content that connects with patients on a human level.

   Prompt Example:
   - "Develop a series of Instagram stories featuring real patients who share their experiences managing a chronic illness, like [Disease Name]. Maintaining a helpful and encouraging tone highlights how patients live fulfilling lives despite their condition.
   - Encourage user-generated content by prompting viewers to share their tips and experiences using a relevant hashtag."
2. **Leveraging Humor to Raise Awareness**:
   - **Challenge**: Serious health topics can be difficult to approach on social media.
   - **Solution**: Use prompts to generate content that educates in a lighthearted and humorous way.

   Prompt Example:

   "Create a series of short funny videos for TikTok that debunk common myths and misconceptions surrounding [Health Topic]. Partner with social media influencers known for their health and wellness content to deliver the information engagingly.

Maintain a balance between humor and accuracy, ensuring the content is informative and medically sound."

3. **Utilizing Interactive Elements to Boost Engagement**:
    - **Challenge**: Static social media posts can struggle to capture audience attention.
    - **Solution**: Use prompts to generate content that encourages interaction.

    Prompt Example:

    "Develop a Facebook poll asking users about their biggest challenges in managing [Disease Name]. Based on the poll results, create a follow-up post with practical tips and resources addressing those challenges. Encourage further engagement by hosting a session with a healthcare professional specializing in the condition."

4. **Harnessing the Power of Visuals:**
    - **Challenge**: People are likelier to stop and engage with visually appealing content.
    - **Solution**: Use prompts to generate visually compelling social media posts.
    - **Prompt Example**:

    "Create a series of eye-catching infographics for Twitter that explain the benefits of [Medication Name] in a visually clear and concise way. Use contrasting colors, simple icons, and data visualizations to communicate the information effectively. Maintain a consistent brand identity by incorporating your brand colors and logo into the infographics.

5. **Celebrating Milestones and Holidays**:
    - **Challenge**: Social media is all about staying relevant and timely.

    Prompt Example:

    "Develop a social media campaign for World Health Day, focusing on the importance of early detection and prevention of [Disease Name]. Partner with a relevant patient advocacy group and create educational posts highlighting available screening options and risk factors. Encourage user-generated content by asking followers to share their stories of overcoming the condition using a specific hashtag."

Remember, these are just a few examples. The best prompts will be tailored to your specific brand, target audience, and social media platform. By experimenting with different prompt types and tracking audience engagement, you can refine your approach and create social media content that educates and fosters community and trust around your pharma brand.

4.4 Exercise: Write Prompts to Create Brand Taglines for GlucoWell

Here are some exercises to help you write prompts for generating GlucoWell's brand Tagline:

1. **Core Values and Brand Identity**:
   - **Start by identifying GlucoWell's Core Values**: What fundamental principles guide the brand? (e.g., empowerment, balance, innovation, etc.).
   - **Consider GlucoWell's Target Audience**: Who are you trying to reach? What are their needs and desires? (For example, adults with Type 2 diabetes seek a more manageable approach to blood sugar control.)

   Prompt Example:

   "Generate a tagline for GlucoWell, a brand that empowers patients with Type 2 diabetes to take control of their health. Focus on keywords like 'empowerment,' 'glycemic balance,' and 'living well with diabetes.' The tagline should be clear, concise, and memorable."
2. **Emotional Connection**:
   - **Think about the emotions you want the tagline to evoke** (e.g., hope, confidence, control).

   Prompt Example:

   "Develop a tagline for GlucoWell that inspires hope and optimism for patients with Type 2 diabetes. Use keywords like 'brighter future,' 'healthy lifestyle,' and 'GlucoWell—Your partner on the path to glycemic balance."
3. **Differentiation**:
   - **What sets GlucoWell apart from other diabetes medications?** Highlight this unique selling proposition (USP) in the tagline.

Prompt Example:

"Create a tagline for GlucoWell that emphasizes its innovative approach to diabetes management. Focus on keywords like 'revolutionary,' 'effective,' and 'taking control of your diabetes.' The tagline should convey a sense of innovation and progress compared to traditional methods."

4. **Call to Action**:
   - **Consider introducing a subtle call to action in the tagline to encourage engagement with your brand.**

   Prompt Example:

   "Develop a tagline for GlucoWell that motivates patients to take charge of their diabetes management. Use keywords like 'start your journey,' 'embrace a healthier you,' and 'GlucoWell – Manage your diabetes, live your life."

Additional Tips:

- **Keep it Short and Sweet**. Aim for a tagline under ten words for optimal impact.
- **Consider Rhyme or Rhythm**. A catchy tagline is more likely to be remembered.
- **Test your taglines with your target audience**. Get feedback to see which ones resonate most effectively.

Using these exercises and prompts as a springboard, you can generate a variety of creative taglines that capture the essence of the GlucoWell brand and resonate with your target audience. Remember, the best tagline will be unique and memorable and effectively communicate GlucoWell's core values and mission to empower patients with Type 2 diabetes to achieve glycemic balance.

4.5 Social Media Posts for GlucoWell Targeting Different Audience Segments (e.g., Patients, Caregivers)

Here are some exercises to craft social media prompts for GlucoWell targeting different audience segments, such as patients with Type 2 diabetes and their caregivers:

A. **For Patients with Type 2 Diabetes**:

- **Platform**: Instagram
- **Target Audience**: Young Adults (18-45)
- **Goal**: Raise awareness about GlucoWell and its benefits in a relatable and informative way.

Prompt:

"Create a series of engaging Instagram posts for GlucoWell featuring young adults managing Type 2 diabetes. Use a lighthearted and informative tone. Showcase how GlucoWell seamlessly integrates into their active lifestyles, allowing them to maintain control of their condition without sacrificing their passions. Incorporate eye-catching visuals and short video snippets to capture attention. Include a clear call to action, such as 'Learn more about GlucoWell and take charge of your diabetes!' And a link to the GlucoWell website."

Platform: Facebook

- **Target Audience**: Middle-aged adults (46+)
- **Goal**: Provide educational content about managing Type 2 diabetes and highlight how GlucoWell can support patients.

Prompt:

"Develop a series of Facebook posts for GlucoWell, addressing common challenges faced by middle-aged adults with Type 2 diabetes, such as maintaining healthy eating habits or dealing with medication adherence. Offer practical tips and resources emphasizing how GlucoWell can help achieve glycemic balance. Maintain a clear and concise tone, using visuals like infographics or charts to enhance understanding.

Encourage audience engagement by asking questions and inviting comments on related topics."

B. **For Caregivers of Patients with Type 2 Diabetes**:

- **Platform**: Facebook Support Group
- **Target Audience**: Caregivers seeking information and support
- **Goal**: Offer resources and guidance to caregivers on supporting their loved ones with Type 2 diabetes.

Prompt:

"Create a series of empathetic and informative posts for a Facebook support group dedicated to caregivers of patients with Type 2 diabetes. Acknowledge caregivers' challenges and provide practical tips for managing daily routines, medication schedules, and emotional well-being. Highlight how GlucoWell can help alleviate some of the burden by simplifying diabetes management. Maintain a supportive and compassionate tone, fostering community within the group. Encourage caregivers to share their experiences and ask questions for peer-to-peer support.

Additional Consideratons:

- Tailor the language and content to the specific platform.
- Use relevant hashtags to increase reach and engagement. (e.g., #Type2Diabetes #DiabetesManagement #GlucoWell
- Respond to comments and messages promptly to build relationships with your audience.

- Track your results and adjust your social media strategy based on what resonates best with your target audience.

By following these prompts and continuously refining your approach, you can leverage social media to create a strong online presence for GlucoWell, connect with patients and caregivers on a deeper level, and establish GlucoWell as a trusted brand that empowers individuals with Type 2diabetes to manage their condition and live fulfilling lives.

CHAPTER

5

Prompt Engineering for Market Research and Competitive Analysis

Market research and competitive analysis are crucial to the pharmaceutical industry's success. However, traditional methods of gathering data and analyzing trends can be time-consuming and resource-intensive. Here's how prompt engineering with large language models (LLMs) can revolutionize this process for pharmaceutical companies.

1. **Identifying Market Trends and Patient Needs**:
    - **Challenge**: Traditional market research often relies on surveys and focus groups, which can be expensive and limited in scope.
    - **Solution**: Utilize prompts to generate insights from vast amounts of online data.

    Prompt Example:

    "Analyze social media conversations, online forums, and patient reviews to identify emerging trends and unmet needs related to [Therapeutic Area]. Focus on keywords like 'treatment challenges,' 'medication side effects,' and 'desired outcomes.' Generate a report summarizing the findings and highlighting areas where pharmaceutical companies can develop innovative solutions to address patient needs."

2. **Understanding Competitor Strategies and Products**:
   - **Challenge**: Staying up-to-date on competitor activities and product pipelines can take time and effort through traditional methods.

   Prompt Example:

   "Develop a comprehensive analysis of [Competitor Company]'s recent patent filings and clinical trial announcements. Identify potential new drugs in development, their targeted indications, and their potential impact on the [Therapeutic Area] market.

   Summarize the analysis clearly and concisely, highlighting potential opportunities and threats to GlucoWell's market position."

3. **Generating Market Landscape Reports**:
   - **Challenge**: Creating detailed reports on market size, growth projections, and key players can be laborious.

   Prompt Example:

   "Generate a comprehensive market research report on the global diabetes medication market. Include market size data, medication type segmentation, and regional trends. Analyze growth projections for the next five years, focusing on factors like the increasing prevalence of diabetes and emerging technologies. Identify key players in the market and their market shares. Present the findings in a visually appealing format with charts, graphs, and key takeaways".

   Benefits of Prompt Engineering for Pharma:

   - **Cost-Effectiveness**: LLMs can analyze vast amounts of data in a shorter timeframe than traditional methods.
   - **Scalability**: Quickly generate insights from diverse data sources, including social media, news articles, and scientific publications.

- **Data-Driven Strategies**: Make informed decisions based on real-world data and trends, not just internal projections.
- **Identify New Opportunities**: Discover new market niches and patient needs to drive innovation and product development.
- **Gain a Competitive Edge**: Monitor competitor activities and anticipate future trends.

Limitations to Consider:

- **Data Quality**: The quality of insights generated depends on the quality and accuracy of the data used.
- **Human Expertise is Still Crucial**: LLMs complement, not replace, the need for human expertise in interpreting data and making strategic decisions.
- **Bias and Ethics**: Ensure prompts are carefully crafted to avoid generating biased or misleading information.

Conclusion

Prompt engineering with LLMs is a powerful tool for pharmaceutical companies to conduct deeper market research and competitive analysis. By leveraging vast online data, pharmaceutical companies can gain valuable insights into patient needs, competitor strategies, and emerging trends. This allows them to make informed decisions, develop innovative solutions, and gain a competitive edge in the ever-evolving pharmaceutical market.

5.1 Using Prompts to Analyze Patient Sentiment and Online Conversations

Understanding patient sentiment and the online conversations they have is crucial for the pharmaceutical industry. Here's how prompt engineering can be harnessed to gain valuable insights:

1. **Identifying Patient Concerns and Frustrations**:
   - **Challenge**: Traditionally, gathering patient feedback relies on surveys or advisory boards, which may not capture the breadth of online discussions.
   - **Solution**: Use prompts to analyze patient sentiment expressed online.

   Prompt Example:

   "Analyze recent social media posts and online forums related to [Medication Name]. Focus on identifying negative sentiments and keywords expressing concerns or frustrations with the medication. Categorize these concerns by themes (e.g., side effects, efficacy, access issues). Generate a report summarizing the findings and highlighting areas where GlucoWell can address these concerns through improved patient education, communication strategies, or product development."
2. **Monitoring Treatment Perceptions and Brand Reputation**:
   - **Challenge**: Gauging public perception of a new treatment or brand awareness can be challenging through traditional methods.

   Prompt Example:

   "Analyze online news articles, blog posts, and social media mentions related to the recent launch of [New Diabetes Medication]. Track the sentiment of these discussions and identify key themes regarding perceived effectiveness, safety profile, and potential patient benefits. Evaluate the overall brand reputation of the medication and identify areas for improvement in communication or public perception."

3. **Understanding Patient Journeys and Needs**:
   - **Challenge**: Traditional methods may not provide a holistic view of the patient journey and their challenges.

   Prompt Example:

   "Analyze online patient communities, blogs, and social media discussions about living with [Disease Name]. Identify common themes and challenges patients face throughout their diagnosis, treatment, and daily management. Focus on keywords like 'diagnosis experience,' 'treatment adherence,' and 'emotional well-being.' Generate a report outlining the different stages of the patient journey and their unmet needs at each stage. Use these insights to inform patient support programs, develop educational materials, and design products or services that cater to their needs."

Benefits of Using Prompts for Patient Sentiment Analysis:

- **Real-Time Insights**: Monitor ongoing conversations and identify emerging trends in patient sentiment.
- **Unbiased Data**: Analyze more opinions than traditional methods, potentially revealing hidden trends.
- **Cost-Effective**: Leverage LLMs to analyze vast amounts of data without incurring high research costs.
- **Deeper Understanding**: Gain insights beyond explicit feedback, capturing emotions and underlying needs.
- **Improved Patient Engagement**: Utilize these insights to tailor communication strategies and develop solutions that resonate with patients.

Limitaitons to Consider:

- **Data Quality**: The accuracy of results depends on the quality and representativeness of online data sources.
- **Privacy Concerns**: Ensure compliance with data privacy regulations when collecting and analyzing online conversations.
- **Focus on Intent**: LLMs may not always accurately interpret the intent behind online language, requiring human oversight.

Conclusion

Prompt engineering is a powerful tool for pharmaceutical companies to gain valuable insights into patient sentiment and online conversations. By analyzing this data, companies can identify patient concerns, monitor brand perception, understand the patient journey, and develop innovative solutions that cater to patient needs. This ultimately leads to improved patient care, a stronger brand reputation, and a competitive edge in the market.

5.2 Generating Competitive Intelligence Reports with AI

Competitive intelligence (CI) is vital for pharmaceutical companies to stay ahead of the curve. AI, particularly prompt engineering, offers a powerful tool to automate data collection and analysis and generate comprehensive CI reports. Here is how it works:

1. **Tracking Competitor Pipelines and Clinical Trials**:
   - **Challenge**: Traditionally, monitoring competitor pipelines involves manually sifting through news articles, press releases, and clinical trial registries.
   - **AI Solution**: Prompt engineering streamlines this process.

   Prompt Example:

   "Develop a comprehensive report on [Competitor company]'s clinical trial pipeline.

   Utilize data from clinicaltrials.gov and other relevant sources. Focus on trials in Phase 2 or later stages, targeting therapeutic areas of [GlucoWell's Focus Areas]. Analyze the trials by drug target, mechanism of action, and potential indications. Generate a report comparing the competitor's pipeline to GlucoWell's current development efforts and highlighting potential threats or opportunities."

2. **Analyzing Patent Landscape and Intellectual Property (IP)**:
   - **Challenge**: Analyzing patent filings manually and assessing competitor IP landscapes can be time-consuming and resource-intensive.

   Prompt Example:

   "Analyze recent patent filings from key competitors in the diabetes treatment space. Identify novel drug formulations, delivery mechanisms, or technologies related to blood sugar control. Assess the potential impact of these patents on GlucoWell's current and future product development. Generate a report summarizing the findings and recommending strategies to navigate the competitive landscape while protecting GlucoWell's intellectual property."

3. **Monitoring Market Trends and Competitor Marketing Strategies**:

    - **Challenge**: Staying updated on competitor marketing tactics and industry trends can be challenging without a dedicated team.

    Prompt Example:

    "Analyze recent social media campaigns and online advertising strategies employed by major players in the diabetes medication market. Identify key messaging themes, target audiences, and tactics to promote competing medications. Compare these strategies to GlucoWell's current marketing approach and identify areas for improvement or differentiation. Generate a report outlining competitor marketing trends and recommending adjustments to GlucoWell's marketing strategy to maximize reach and brand impact."

Benefits of using AI for Competitive Intelligence Reports:

- **Efficacy and Speed**: AI automates data collection and analysis, generating reports significantly faster than traditional methods.
- **Enhanced Accuracy**: Streamlined data processing reduces the risk of human error and ensures consistent reporting.
- **Deeper Insights**: AI can analyze larger datasets and identify intricate patterns or potential risks invisible to manual analysis.
- **Data-Driven Decisions**: Reports based on factual data support informed decision-making for product development, market positioning, and competitive strategies.

- **Continuous Monitoring**: AI can continuously monitor competitor activities and market trends, keeping GlucoWell well-prepared for future challenges and opportunities.

Limitations to Consider:

- **Data Quality**: The accuracy of AI-generated reports depends on the quality and reliability of the data sources used.
- **Human Expertise**: While AI automates tasks, human expertise remains crucial for interpreting data, identifying trends, and drawing strategic conclusions.
- **Bias Mitigation**: Prompt engineering design requires careful consideration to avoid generating biased reports that favor specific competitors or data sources.

Conclusion

Prompt engineering with AI offers pharmaceutical companies a transformative approach to generating comprehensive CI reports. By automating data analysis and leveraging larger datasets, AI provides valuable insights into competitor activities, market trends, and IP landscapes. This enables pharmaceutical companies to make informed decisions about product development, market positioning, and staying ahead of the competition in the ever-evolving pharmaceutical landscape.

5.3 Exercises: Develop Prompts to:

- **Analyze Public Perception of Diabetes Medications on Social Media**
- **Identify Key Differences Between GlucoWell and Competitor Brands**

Analyze Public Perception of Diabetes Medications on Social Media

Social media provides a goldmine of data on public perception of diabetes medications. Here are some prompts to leverage prompt engineering and analyze this data effectively:

1. **Sentiment Analysis:**

   Prompt Example #1:

   "Analyze recent social media posts (Twitter, Facebook, Instagram) mentioning [Diabetes Medication Name]. Identify the overall sentiment (positive, negative, neutral) expressed towards the medication. Focus on keywords related to effectiveness, side effects, and user experience. Generate a report summarizing the sentiment distribution and highlighting the most frequently mentioned themes (e.g., dosge concerns, positive impact on blood sugar control).

   Prompt Example #2:

   "Compare the sentiment expressed towards [Diabetes Medication A] and [Diabetes Medication B] on social media. Identify the key factors influencing user perception of each medication. Generate a report highlighting the strengths and weaknesses of each medication based on public perception."

2. **Identifying Common Concerns and Benefits:**

   Prompt Example:

   "Analyze social media discussions related to injectable diabetes medications. Extract the most frequently mentioned concerns and anxieties users have about injectable medications (e.g., pain, needles, adherence). Identify positive aspects and benefits users highlight about injectable medications (e.g., rapid action, improved control).

Generate a report summarizing these findings and suggesting communication strategies to address user concerns and emphasize the advantages of injectable medications for appropriate patients."

3. **Highlight Positive Aspects:**

   Prompt Example:

   "Analyze social media discussions related to diabetes medications. Extract the most frequently mentioned positive aspects and user experiences (e.g., improved blood sugar control, increased energy levels, and ease of use). Generate a report summarizing these benefits and consider using them for targeted marketing campaigns for appropriate audiences."

4. **Understanding Patient Experiences and Support Networks"**

   Prompt Example:

   "Analyze social media posts using hashtags like #Type2Diabetes and #DiabetesCommunity. Identify themes related to managing diabetes with medication.

   Focus on keywords like 'daily routine,' 'medication adherence,' and 'support groups.' Generate a report describing patients' challenges and successes in managing their diabetes with medication. Highlight examples of online support networks and resources that patients find helpful."

5. **Patient Experiences and Support Networks:**

   - **Understanding Patient Journeys:**

   Prompt Example:

   "Analyze social media posts using hashtags like #Type2Diabetes or #DiabetesCommunity. Identify themes related to starting, managing, and transitioning between different diabetes medications. Focus on keywords like 'medication switch,' 'adherence challenges,' and 'emotional impact.' Generate a report outlining the challenges and successes patients face with various medications."

- **Exploring Support Networks**:

  "Analyze how patients utilize social media to find support related to diabetes medications. Identify online communities, support groups, and patient advocacy organizations active on social media platforms. Generate a report summarizing these support networks and explore potential collaborations to reach a wider audience."

6. **Tracking Brand Awareness and Marketing Effectiveness:**

   - **Tracking Brand Perception:**

     Prompt Example:

     "Monitor social media mentions of GlucoWell in the past month. Analyze the reach and engagement of recent marketing campaigns. Identify the types of content resonating most with the target audience. Generate a report evaluating the effectiveness of GlucoWell's social media strategy and recommending potential improvements for future campaigns."

   - **Competitor Analysis**:

     Prompt Example:

     "Compare the social media presence of several diabetes medication brands. Analyze their use of hashtags, content formats, and audience engagement strategies. Identify best practices and potential areas for differentiation for a specific brand (e.g., GlucoWell)."

Additional Tips:

- Refine your prompts based on specific research goals.
- Utilize relevant keywords and hashtags to focus the analysis.

- Consider demographic filters to segment the data by user age, location, etc.
- Combine sentiment analysis with topic modeling to understand the context behind user opinions. Complement AI insights with human analysis to understand public perception better.

Using these prompts as a starting point and continually refining your approach, you can leverage the power of social media data to gain valuable insights into public perception of diabetes medications. This information can be used to:

- Improve communication strategies to address patient concerns and educate the public.
- Develop targeted marketing campaigns that resonate with specific audience segments.
- Refine product development based on user needs and preferences.

Identify potential areas for differentiation in the competitive landscape. Remember, social media analysis is an ongoing process. By continuously monitoring public perceptions and adapting your approach, you can ensure that your brand messaging resonates with patients and positions your diabetes medication solution as a valuable tool for managing the condition.

Identify Key Differences Between GlucoWell and Competitor Brands

Prompts to Identify Key Differentiators Between GlucoWell and Competitor Brands:

1. **Value Proposition and Target Audience**:
   - **Prompt Example**:

     "Analyze competitor marketing materials and social media presence to understand their target audiences and value propositions. Identify the key benefits they emphasize for their diabetes medications. Compare how these align or differ from GlucoWell's focus on empowering patients with Type 2 diabetes to achieve glycemic balance and live fulfilling lives."

2. **Product Features and Innovation**:
   - **Prompt Example**:

   "Develop a comprehensive comparison chart of GlucoWell's features (e.g., dosage forms, delivery mechanisms, unique ingredients) with competitor medications. Include information on any patents or proprietary technologies associated with GlucoWell.

   Identify areas where GlucoWell offers distinct advantages or potential for innovation compared to its competitors."

3. **Patient Support and User Experience**:
   - **Prompt Example**:

   "Analyze online reviews and forums to compare patient experiences with GlucoWell and competitor medications. Focus on themes related to medication effectiveness, side effects, ease of use, and customer service. Identify areas where GlucoWell excels in providing a positive and supportive user experience for patients managing Type 2 diabetes."

4. **Brand Image and Messaging**:
   - **Prompt Example**:

   "Develop a comparative analysis of GlucoWell's brand image and messaging compared to key competitors. Analyze the language, visuals, and tone used in marketing materials and social media content. Identify unique aspects of GlucoWell's brand personality and how it resonates with patients seeking solutions for managing their diabetes."

5. **Pricing and Accessibility**:
   - **Prompt Example**:

     "Compare the pricing and affordability of GlucoWell with competitor medications. Consider factors like co-pay assistance programs, insurance coverage, and availability through online pharmacies or telehealth consultations. Identify how GlucoWell can offer greater accessibility and cost-effectiveness for patients managing their condition."

Additional Tips:

- **Focus on specific competitor brands** relevant to GlucoWell's market position.
- **Utilize relevant keywords and hashtags** to gather targeted information from online sources.
- **Gather qualitative data** (patient testimonials, reviews) alongside quantitative data (market share statistics).
- **Analyze the strengths and weaknesses** of both Glucowell and its competitors to identify clear differentiation points.
- **Consider future trends** in diabetes management and how GlucoWell can position itself at the forefront.

By following these prompts and continuously refining your approach, you can gain valuable insights into how GlucoWell compares to its competitors. This information can be used to develop targeted marketing strategies, refine product offerings, and position GlucoWell as the most attractive and effective solution for patients seeking to manage their Type 2 diabetes effectively.

Part III. The Prompt Engineering Workbook for GlucoWell Branding

6. Building a Cohesive Brand Narrative with Prompts
7. Prompt Engineering for Content Marketing and Advertising
8. Optimizing Your Prompts to Maximum Impact

Harnessing the Power of AI for Effective Pharma Marketing

Welcome to Part 3 of this comprehensive guide, which explores the practical application of prompt engineering tailored to GlucoWell's branding initiatives. This workbook is designed to equip you with the tools and strategies to create compelling content that resonates with your target audience, patients with Type 2 diabetes.

The Importance of Tailored Content

Patients are inundated with information from various sources in today's digital age. Relevant, informative, and personalized content is essential to standing out and capturing attention. Prompt engineering allows you to generate content tailored to the specific needs and interests of GlucoWell's target audience.

Key Areas of Focus:

- **Patient Education**: Develop informative and engaging content that educates patients about Type 2 diabetes, its management, and the benefits of GlucoWell.
- **Brand Storytelling**: Craft compelling narratives highlighting GlucoWell's mission, values, and success stories.
- **Patient Engagement**: Create interactive content that encourages patients to participate and share their experiences.
- **Social Media Content**: Develop engaging posts that resonate with your target audience and drive traffic to your website.
- **Email Marketing**: Create personalized email campaigns that deliver valuable information and encourage patients to take action.

Benefits of Using Prompt Engineering:

- **Efficiency**: Prompt engineering can save time and resources by automating content creation.

- **Consistency**: It helps ensure your content aligns with GlucoWell's brand voice and messaging.
- **Personalization** allows you to create content tailored to patients' needs and preferences.
- **Creativity**: Prompt engineering can inspire new ideas and creative approaches to content creation.

The following chapters will provide specific prompts and examples to help you apply prompt engineering to your GlucoWell's Branding efforts. By following these guidelines and leveraging the power of AI, you can create content that resonates with patients, drives engagement, and improves health outcomes.

CHAPTER 6

Building a Cohesive Brand Narrative with Prompts

Crafting a compelling brand narrative is crucial in the competitive world of pharmaceuticals. It goes beyond product features and establishes an emotional connection with patients and healthcare providers (HCPs). Here's how prompt engineering can be harnessed to build a strong narrative for pharmaceutical companies.

1. **Defining Your Brand Story**:
   - **Mission and Values**: What is your company's core purpose? What principles guide your work?
   - **Prompt Example**:

   "Develop a concise and impactful brand story for GlucoWell, a brand focused on empowering patients with Type 2 diabetes. Highlight GlucoWell's mission to revolutionize diabetes management by providing innovative solutions and unwavering support. Emphasize the company's values of patient-centricity, scientific rigor, and a commitment to improving lives."
2. **Identifying Your Target Audience**:
   - Who are you trying to reach with your brand narrative? Patients? HCPs? Tailor your story accordingly.
   - **Prompt Example**:

     "Craft a patient-centric narrative for GlucoWell, focusing on the journey of a person with Type 2 diabetes who takes control of their condition with the help of GlucoWell and its ongoing support system. Evoke hope, empowerment, and a return to fulfilling life."

3. **Showcasing Expertise and Innovation**:
   - Highlight your scientific background and commitment to R&D.
   - **Prompt Example**:

   "Develop a compelling narrative that showcases GlucoWell's dedication to scientific innovation. Describe the journey of GlucoWell's development, from initial research to clinical trials, emphasizing the team's expertise and commitment to bringing a safe and effective solution to patients with Type 2 diabetes.

4. **Building Trust and Transparency**:
   - Be upfront about the benefits and potential limitations of your product.
   - Prompt Example:

   "Craft a transparent narrative for GlucoWell, acknowledging the challenges of managing Type 2 diabetes. Position GlucoWell as a reliable partner in this journey, offering effective medication, educational resources, and ongoing support to empower patients to achieve glycemic balance."

5. **Integrating Patient Testimonials**:
   - Leverage the power of real-life stories to connect with your audience.
   - **Prompt Example**:

   "Develop a series of patient testimonials that weave into GlucoWell's brand narrative.

   Showcase how GlucoWell has positively impacted the lives of people with Type 2 diabetes. Focus on improved health, increased confidence, and renewed control over their health condition."

Benefits of Prompt Engineering for Brand Narratives:

- **Clarity and Focus**: Prompts ensure your narrative stays on message and resonates with your target audience.

- **Emotional Connection**: Evokes empathy and understanding to build trust with patients and HCPs.
- **Consistency**: Maintains a consistent narrative across all communication channels.
- **Data-Driven Insights**: Integrates patients and market research to inform your narrative.
- **Adaptability**: Tailors your narrative to different audiences and evolving market dynamics.

Limitations to Consider

- **Authenticity**: Ensure your narrative is genuine and reflects the company's values.
- **Overpromising**: Avoid unrealistic claims that can erode trust.
- **Target Audience Fit:** Tailor your narrative to resonate with your audience's needs and perspectives.

Conclusion

Prompt engineering offers pharma companies a powerful tool for building a cohesive brand narrative. By crafting a compelling story highlighting your mission, scientific expertise, and commitment to patient well-being, you can establish a strong emotional connection with your target audience and position your company as a leader in the healthcare space.

6.1 Crafting the GlucoWell Brand Story: Mission, Vision and Values

Here is how to craft a compelling brand story for GlucoWell, focusing on its mission, vision, and values:

Mission:

- **Focus on GlucoWell's Core Purpose**: What problem are you solving for patients with Type 2 diabetes?
- **Example**: "To empower patients with Type 2 diabetes to take control of their health by providing innovative treatment solutions and comprehensive support systems, enabling them to achieve glycemic balance and live fulfilling lives."

Vision:

- **Paint a Picture of the Future State GlucoWell Aspires to Create:** How will GlucoWell impact the lives of patients and the diabetes treatment landscape?
- **Example**: "To become a leading force in revolutionizing diabetes management, offering patients with Type 2 diabetes the freedom and confidence to live their lives to the fullest, free from the limitations of their condition."

Values:

- **Define the Core Principles that Guide GlucoWell's Actions and Decision-Making:** These should resonate with patients and healthcare providers (HCPs).
- **Examples**:
- **Patient-Centricity**: Prioritizes the needs and well-being of patients in everything it does.
- **Scientific Rigor**: Committed to developing and delivering safe, effective, evidence-based solutions.

- **Empowerment**: Believes in equipping patients with the knowledge and tools to manage their diabetes effectively.
- **Innovation**: Dedicated to continuous research and development to advance diabetes treatment.
- **Collaboration**: Fosters partnerships with healthcare providers to deliver optimal patient care.

Weaving the Narrative:

Once you have a clear mission, vision, and values, you can weave them into a cohesive brand narrative. This narrative should be present across all communication channels, from website content and marketing materials to patient interactions and HCP outreach.

Here's an example of how these elements might be integrated into a narrative:

GlucoWell is committed to empowering patients with Type 2 diabetes to take control of their health. It understands the challenges of managing this condition and is dedicated to providing innovative treatment solutions and unwavering support. Driven by scientific rigor and a passion for patient well-being, GlucoWell strives to revolutionize diabetes management and create a future where patients can live fulfilling lives free from the limitations of their condition. Through collaboration with healthcare providers and a commitment to ongoing research, GlucoWell constantly seeks advancements to empower patients to live well with Type 2 diabetes.

By crafting a clear and compelling brand story that reflects your mission, vision, and values, GlucoWell can establish a strong emotional connection with patients and HCPs, positioning itself as a trusted partner in diabetes management.

Prompts to Craft GlucoWell's Brand Narrative: Mission, Vision, and Values

1. **Mission**:
   - **Prompt Example**:

   "Describe the ideal future state for patients with Type 2 diabetes who utilize GlucoWell Solutions. How does GlucoWell empower them to manage their condition and achieve their glycemic balance?"
2. **Vision**:
   - **Prompt Example**:

   "Imagine a world where diabetes management is significantly improved. How GlucoWell contributes to this vision and how it impacts the lives of patients and the healthcare landscape?"
3. **Values**:
   - **Prompt Example 1**:

   "Identify the key qualities that differentiate GlucoWell from competitors. What core principles guide GlucoWell's patient care and product development approach?"
   - **Prompt Example 2**:

   "Think about the emotional connection you want to build with patients. What values resonate with them in managing Type 2 diabetes?"
4. **Narrative Integration**:
   - **Prompt Example**:

   "Develop a compelling brand story that weaves GlucoWell's mission, vision, and values together. Highlight how GlucoWell addresses patient needs, leverages scientific expertise, and contributes to a brighter future for managing Type 2 diabetes?"

Additional Tips:

- **Conduct Workshops** with internal stakeholders (scientists, marketers, patient advocates) to brainstorm ideas.

- **Gather Patient Insights** through surveys or focus groups to understand their needs and aspirations.
- **Research Competitor Messaging** to identify differentiation opportunities to your brand narrative.
- **Refine Your Prompts** based on the insights gathered to create a clear and concise brand story.

Using these prompts as a starting point and iteratively refining your approach, you can develop a strong brand narrative that resonates with your target audience and positions GlucoWell as a leader in the diabetes management space.

6.2 Developing a Compelling Brand Voice and Tone with AI

In the competitive world of pharmaceuticals, crafting a distinct brand voice and tone is crucial for establishing trust and connecting with patients and healthcare providers (HCPs). Here's how AI, specifically prompt engineering, can be harnessed to develop a compelling brand voice and tone for pharma companies.

Understanding Your Brand Identity:

AI can't replace human creativity, but it can assist in defining your brand identity:

- **Analyze Existing Materials**: Use prompts to analyze your website content, marketing materials, and social media interactions to identify existing brand voice and tone elements.
- **Prompt Example**:

  "Analyze the top 10 website pages and recent social media posts from [Pharma Company Name]. Identify keywords and phrases used to describe the company's products and services. Categorize these items based on tone (e.g., informative, empathetic, authoritative)."

Understanding Your Audience:

AI can help you tailor your voice and tone to resonate with your target audience.

- **Patient Personas**: Develop patient personas with distinct demographics, needs, and communication preferences.
- **Prompt Example**:

  "For a patient persona of a 55-year-old woman newly diagnosed with Type 2 Diabetes, generate sample messages in different tones (informative, supportive, empowering) explaining the benefits of a new medication."
- **HCP Insights**: Analyze industry publications and online forums to understand how HCPs prefer to receive information from pharma companies.

- **Prompt Example**:

  "Analyze recent articles in medical journals and online discussions between HCPs. Identify the preferred communication style (formal, concise, data-driven) for conveying results".

Crafting Your Brand Voice with Prompts:

- **Clarity and Concision**:
- **Prompt Example**:

  "Develop a series of social media posts about the benefits of a new cholesterol medication. Emphasize clarity and conciseness while maintaining an informative and patient-friendly tone."
- **Empathy and Support**:
- **Prompt Example**:

  "Craft a series of email templates for a patient support program addressing common concerns and anxieties associated with a specific medication. Prioritize a supportive and empathetic tone while providing accurate information."
- **Authority and Expertise**:
- **Prompt Example**:

  "Develop a press release announcing the successful completion of a Phase 3 clinical trial for a new cancer treatment. Maintain a confident and authoritative tone while adhering to scientific accuracy and ethical communication practices."

Benefits of Using AI for Brand Voice and Tone:

- **Consistency**: Ensure a consistent voice and tone across all communication channels.
- **Efficiency**: Quickly generate and test different voice and tone options.
- **Patient-Centricity**: Develop messaging that resonates with your target audience.

- **Data-Driven Insights**: Utilize patient and market research to inform your voice and tone.
- **Evolving Voice**: Continuously refine your voice and tone based on audience feedback and market trends.

Limitations to Consider

- **Human Oversight**: AI is a tool, not a replacement for human creativity and strategic decision-making.
- **Brand Authority**: AI-generated content requires human review to ensure it aligns with your brand's core values.
- **Emotional Nuance:** AI may struggle to capture the full spectrum of human emotions that can strengthen brand voice.

Examples:

- **Informative and Empowering:** "At [Company Name], we believe in providing patients with the knowledge and tools they need to manage their health effectively." (Empowering patients with Type 2 diabetes)
- **Supportive and Encouraging**: "We understand the challenges of living with a chronic condition, and we are here to support you every step of the way." (Cancer Treatment Support Program)
- **Optimistic and Motivational**: "With [Medication Name], you can significantly improve your health and well-being." (New cholesterol medication launch)

Conclusion

AI offers a valuable tool for pharma companies to develop a compelling brand voice and tone. By leveraging prompt engineering to analyze existing materials, understanding your audience, and generating creative content options, you can craft a unique voice that resonates with patients and HCPs, fosters trust, and position your brand as a leader in the healthcare space. However, remember that AI is a support system, not a replacement for human creativity and strategic direction in establishing your brand voice.

6.3 Exercises: Write Prompts to:

- **Define GlucoWell Brand Story Elements**
- **Establish GlucoWell's Brand Voice and Tone with AI**

1. **Define GlucoWell's Brand Story Elements**: Let's focus on prompts to define GlucoWell's brand story elements:

   A. **Mission**:

   - **Prompt Example**:

   "Imagine a world where patients with Type 2 diabetes have the power to manage their condition effectively and live fulfilling lives. How does GlucoWell contribute to this vision, and what problem is it solving for patients?"

B. **Vision**:

   - **Prompt Example**:

   "What is GlucoWell's ultimate goal in revolutionizing diabetes management?

   How will its solutions empower patients and redefine what it means to live well with Type 2 diabetes?"

C. **Values**:

   - **Prompt Example 1**:

   "Describe the core principles that differentiate GlucoWell from competitors.

   What values guide their approach to patient care and product development?"

   - **Prompt Example 2**:

   "Think about the emotional connection you want to build with patients. What values resonate with them as they navigate their journey with Type 2 diabetes?"

D. Target Audience:

- **Prompt Example**:

"Develop a detailed profile of GlucoWell's ideal patient. Consider demographics, lifestyle, technological preferences, and their current approach to managing Type 2 diabetes."

E. Competitive Landscape:

- **Prompt Example**:

Analyze how GlucoWell's competitors position themselves in the diabetes management space. Identify gaps or unmet needs that GlucoWell's brand story can address."

Crafting the Narrative

- **Prompt Example**:

  "Weave GlucoWell's mission, values, and target audience into a cohesive brand narrative. Highlight how GlucoWell's solutions empower patients, leverage scientific expertise, and contribute to a brighter future for managing Type 2 diabetes."

Additional Tips:

- Conduct workshops with internal stakeholders (scientists, marketers, patient advocates) to brainstorm ideas. Research patient perspectives on diabetes management through surveys or focus groups.
- Analyze competitor messaging to identify differentiation opportunities in GlucoWell's brand story.
- Refine your prompts based on the insights gathered to create a clear and concise brand story.
- Using these prompts as a starting point, you can develop a strong brand story for GlucoWell that resonates with your target audience and positions it as a leader in diabetes management.

2. **Framework for Analyzing Your Competitors' Brand Voice and Tone**: Here is a framework to analyze your competitor's top website pages and social media posts using prompts. This framework will help you identify keywords and phrases and categorize the tone used to describe their products and services.

   - **Analysis Steps**:

   1. **Content Selection**: By analyzing traffc data, identify the top 10 most visited website pages using website analytics tools. Select a representative sample of recent social media posts from various platforms (e.g., Twitter, Facebook, LinkedIn).
   2. **Keyword Phrase Identification**: Review the selected website pages and social media posts. Pay attention to keywords and phrases used to describe the competitor company's products, services, and approaches to diabetes management, for example.
   3. **Tone Categorization**: Classify the keywords and phrases based on their dominant tone. Here's a categorization scheme you can adapt:
      - **Informative**: Facts, statistics, and data-driven statements about products and disease conditions (e.g., "Long-acting insulin for sustained blood sugar control").
      - **Empathetic**: Acknowledges challenges, expresses understanding, and offers support. (e.g., "We understand living with diabetes can be dificult, but you're not alone.")
      - **Authoritative**: Demonstrates expertise, highlights scientific rigor, and emphasizes clinical trial results (e.g., "Our commitment to research has led to innovative diabetes treatment solutions.")

- **Trustworthy**: Emphasizes transparency, ethical practices, and patient safety.

  (e.g., "We are committed to providing patients with safe and effective medications.")
- **Empowering**: Focuses on patient control, self-management, and living a full life with a chronic condition like diabetes (e.g., "Take charge of your diabetes and achieve your health goals.")

Additional Considerations:

- Note the overall sentiment conveyed through the language used.
- Identify any visuals or multimedia elements contributing to the brand's voice and tone.
- Consider how the tone varies depending on the target audience (patients, HCPs, and investors).

Example Output:

Consider, for example, you find after analyzing Novo Nordisk's website pages and social media posts, you might identify keywords like "long-acting insulin," "blood sugar control," "personalized care," "clinical trials," and "patient support." Categorization might reveal a dominant informative tone when describing products, an empathetic tone in posts addressing patient challenges and an authoritative tone when discussing research and development.

By following this framework and analyzing your competitor's communication channels, you can gain valuable insights into their brand voice and tone. This will help you understand how they position themselves within the diabetes management space and how they connect with their target audience.

3. **Prompts to Esbalish GlucoWell's Brand Voice and Tone**:
   - In the competitive world of pharmaceuticals, crafting a

distinct brand voice and tone is crucial for establishing trust and connecting with patients and healthcare providers (HCPs). Here's how AI, specifically prompt engineering, can be harnessed to develop a compelling brand voice and tone for pharmaceutical companies:

F. **Understanding Your Brand Identity**: AI can't replace human creativity, but it can assist in defining your brand identity:

- **Analyze Existing Materials**: Use prompts to analyze your website content, marketing materials, and social media interactions to identify existing brand voice and tone elements.
- **Prompt Example**:

  "Analyze the top 10 website pages and recent social media posts from [Pharma Company Name]. Identify keywords and phrases used to describe the company's products and services. Categorize these terms based on tone (e.g., informative, empathetic, authoritative)."

G. **Understanding Your Audience**: AI can help you tailor your voice and tone to resonate with your target audience.

- **Patient Personas**: Develop patient personas with distinct demographics, needs, and communication preferences.
- **Prompt Example**:

  "For a patient persona of a 55-year-old woman newly diagnosed with Type 2 diabetes, generate sample messages in different tones (informative, supportive, empowering) explaining the benefits of a new medicaiton."
- **HCP Insights**: Analyze industry publications and online forums to understand how HCPs prefer to receive information from pharma companies.
- **Prompt Example**:

  "Analyze recent articles in medical journals and online discussions between HCPs. Identify the preferred communication style (formal, concise, data-driven) for conveying new clinical trial results."

H. Crafting Your Brand Voice with Prompts:

- **Clarity and Concision**:
- **Prompt Example**:

  "Develop a series of social media posts about the benefits of a new cholesterol medication. Emphasize clarity and conciseness while maintaining an informative and patient-friendly tone."

- **Empathy and Support**:
- **Prompt Example**:

  "Craft a series of email templates for a patient support program addressing common concerns and anxieties associated with a specific medication.

  Prioritize a supportive and empathetic tone while providing accurate information."

- **Authority and Expertise**:
- **Prompt Example**:

  "Develop a press release announcing the successful completion of a Phase 3 clinical trial for a new cancer treatment. Maintain a confident and authoritative tone while adhering to scientific accuracy and ethical communication practices."

Benefits of Using AI for Brand Voice and Tone:

- **Consistency**: Ensure a consistent voice and tone across all communication channels.
- **Efficiency**: Quickly generate and test different voice and tone options.
- **Patient-Centricity**: Develop messaging that resonates with your target audience.

- **Data-Driven Insights**: Utilize patient and market research to inform your voice and tone.
- **Evolving Voice**: Continuously refine your voice and tone based on audience feedback and market trends.

Limitations to Consider

- **Human Oversight:** AI is a tool, not a replacement for human creativity and strategic decision-making.
- **Brand Authenticity**: AI-generated content requires human review to ensure it aligns with your brand's core values.
- **Emotional Intelligence**: AI may struggle to capture the full spectrum of human emotions that can strengthen brand voice.

Examples:

- **Informative and Empowering**: "At [Company Name]. We believe in providing patients with the knowledge and tools they need to manage their health effectively." (Empowering Patients with Type 2 Diabetes).
- **Supportive and Encouraging**: "We understand the challenges of living with a chronic condition, and we are here to support you every step of the way." (Cancer Treatment Support Program).
- **Optimistic and Motivational**: "With [Medication Name], you have the potential to achieve significant improvements in your health and well-being." (New Cholesterol Medication Launch).

  AI offers pharma companies a valuable tool for developing a compelling brand voice and tone. By leveraging prompt engineering to analyze existing materials, understand your audience, and generate creative content options, you can craft a unique voice that resonates with patients and HCPs, fosters trust, and positions your brand as a leader in the healthcare space. However, remember AI serves as a support system, not a replacement for human creativity and strategic direction in establishing your brand voice.

4. **Prompts to Develop GlucoWell's Ideal Patient Profile**:
   - **Demographics:**
   - **Age**: 40-60 years old (depending on specific GlucoWell product lines).
   - **Gender**: More likely female, but expanding to include men as well.
   - **Location**: Primarily urban or suburban areas in developed countries.
   - **Socioeconomic Status**: Varied, but focusing on reaching patients with health insurance coverage for medication.
   - **Lifestyle**:
   - Moderately active but may be looking to increase activity levels.
   - Juggles work, family, and social commitments.
   - Time-conscious and values convenience.
   - Increasingly tech-savvy and comfortable using smartphones and health apps.

Diagnosis and Emotional State:

- Recently diagnosed with Type 2 diabetes or looking for a new management solution.
- May be feeling overwhelmed, frustrated, or anxious about their diagnosis and the lifestyle changes required.
- Desires to take control of their health and live a full, active life.
- Seeks trustworthy and reliable information about managing their condition.

Technology Comfort Level:

- Comfortable using smartphones and downloading apps.

- Open to using connected devices (e.g., blood glucose monitors) May need some initial guidance on using new technologies for diabetes management.

Needs and Pain Points:

- Needs clear and concise information about Type 2 diabetes and treatment options.
- Wants a medication that is effective and easy to integrate into their daily routine.
- Seeks support and guidance on healthy living habits (diet, exercise).
- Appreciates tools and resources that help them monitor their glucose levels and track their progress.

Ideal Tone for Communication:

- **Informative and Empowering**: Provide clear and accurate information about GlucoWell and its benefits in managing Type 2 diabetes. Emphasize how GlucoWell empowers patients to take control of their health.
- **Supportive and Encouraging**: Acknowledge the challenges of managing a chronic condition and offer support and encouragement. Highlight success stories and positive outcomes achieved by other GlucoWell users.
- **Motivational and Uplifting**: Use an optimistic and motivating tone to inspire patients to make healthy lifestyle changes and achieve their health goals.
- **Conversational and Approachable**: Avoid overly technical language and maintain a friendly, approachable tone that builds trust and encourages open communication.

Understanding GlucoWell's ideal patient profile and the tone that resonates most effectively with them can help you develop targeted communication strategies that address their needs and concerns. This will allow GlucoWell to connect with patients more deeply, build stronger relationships, and improve patient outcomes.

5. **Developing Sample Social Media Posts Explaining How GlucoWell Helps Manage Type 2 Diabetes**:

Post 1 (Facebook / Instagram)

- **Headline**: Feeling overwhelmed by Type 2 diabetes? GlucoWell can help!
- **Body**: Our medication works by [brief explanation of the mechanism of action, e.g., helping your body produce more insulin or use insulin more effectively]. This can lead to better blood sugar control and a healthier you!

Call to Action: Visit our website (link in bio) to learn more about how GlucoWell can simplify diabetes management. #Type2Diabetes #gGucoWellSolutions#TakeControl.

Post 2 (Twitter)

- **Headline**: GlucoWell: Your partner in managing Type 2 diabetes.
- **Body**: We offer a medication that helps regulate blood sugar by [brief explanation of mechanism of action]. Ask your doctor if GlucoWell is right for you! #GlucoWell #DiabetesManagement #TalkToYourDoctor.

Post 3 (LinkedIn)

- **Headline**: GlucoWell: A New Approach to empowering patients with Type 2 diabetes.
- **Body**: Our innovative medication utilizes [mechanism of action] to support healthy blood sugar levels. We're committed to providing effective solutions and ongoing patient support. #GlucoWell #HealthcareInnovation #Type2DiabetesCare

Additional Tips:

- Include visuals (infographics, short animations) to enhance understanding in Facebook/Instagram posts.
- Maintain consistent branding elements (colors, fonts) across all social media platforms.
- Encourage questions and comments in the posts to foster engagement with your audience.
- Consider using relevant hashtags to increase reach and connect with online communities.

CHAPTER

7

Prompt Engineering for Content Marketing and Advertising

The pharmaceutical industry relies heavily on effective content marketing and advertising to reach healthcare professionals (HCPs) and patients. However, crafting compelling and compliant messages can be challenging. Prompt engineering offers a powerful tool to overcome this hurdle.

This chapter explores how pharmaceutical companies can use prompt engineering to develop engaging content and targeted advertising across various channels.

Benefits of Prompt Engineering in Pharma Marketing:

- **Content Personalization**: Tailor content to specific audiences (HCPs vs. patients) and disease areas.
- **Data-Driven Insights**: Utilize patient data and market research to inform your prompts.
- **Creative Efficiency**: Generate a wider range of content ideas quickly.
- **Compliance Adherence**: Ensure content adheres to strict regulatory guidelines.
- **Brand Consistency**: Maintain a consistent brand voice and tone across all marketing materials.

Examples of Prompt Engineering in Pharma Marketing:

1. **Patient Education Blog Posts**:
    - **Prompt Example**:

      "Develop a blog post for patients with Type 2 diabetes explaining the importance of medication adherence in managing blood sugar levels. Maintain a clear, concise, and informative tone while incorporating inspirational patient stories and practical tips."
2. **Targeted Social Media Ads**:
    - **Prompt Example**:

      "Generate social media ad copy for a new asthma medication, targeting adults experiencing frequent symptoms. Highlight the medication's benefits in reducing symptoms and improving quality of life. Use an empathetic and reassuring tone, with a visual depicting an active lifestyle."
3. **HCP Education Webinars**:
    - **Prompt Example**:

      "Create a script for a webinar educating HCPs about the latest clinical trial results for a new cancer treatment. Ensure the tone is authoritative, data-driven, and emphasizes the treatment's potential for improving patient outcomes."
4. **Interactive Patient Journey Tools**:
    - **Prompt Example**:

      "Develop prompts for an interactive online tool guiding patients with chronic migraines through their treatment journey. The tool should offer personalized recommendations, educational resources, and a supportive tone while remaining HIPAA compliant."

Challenges and Considerations

- **Scientific Accuracy**: Content must be medically accurate and compliant with regulatory guidelines.
- **Human Oversight**: AI-generated content requires human review and editing to ensure factual accuracy and brand alignment.
- **Emotional Nuance**: While AI can generate ideas, human creativity remains crucial for conveying empathy and emotional connection in patient-facing content.

How Pharma Utilizes Prompt Engineering

Pharmaceutical Companies:

- Utilize AI to generate personalized content for HCPs based on their past interactions and areas of interest.
- Employ AI to analyze patient data and develop targeted social media campaigns for specific disease areas.
- Leverage AI to create educational materials for patients undergoing cancer treatment, ensuring clear communication and emotional support.

Conclusion

Prompt engineering offers pharma companies a valuable tool to elevate their content marketing and advertising efforts. By harnessing the power of AI to generate creative ideas, personalize content, and streamline workflows, pharma companies can reach their target audiences with impactful messages that educate, engage, and improve patient outcomes. However, it's crucial to remember that AI serves as a support system, not a replacement for human expertise, medical accuracy, and the importance of building trust with patients and HCPs.

7.1 Generating Website Content for GlucoWell with Prompts

Here are some prompts you can use to generate website content for GlucoWell, focusing on different sections of the website:

1. **Homepage**:
   - **Prompt Example**:

     "Develop compelling website copy for GlucoWell's homepage that clearly explains who they are, what they offer (diabetes management solutions), and the benefits patients can experience using their products. Maintain a warm, approachable tone that emphasizes patient empowerment."
2. **About Us**:
   - **Prompt Example**:

     "Craft informative 'About Us' page for GlucoWell. Highlight the company's mission, values, and commitment to improving the lives of people with Type 2 Diabetes. Briefly showcase the team's scientific expertise and dedication to innovation."
3. **Products**:
   - **Prompt Example**:

     "Generate detailed product page descriptions of GlucoWell's dosage forms. Ensure clarity and accuracy while explaining the medication's mechanism of action for blood sugar control and dosage information. Include disclaimers and a call to action to speak with a doctor."
4. **FAQs**:
   - **Prompt Example**:

     "Develop a comprehensive FAQ section for GlucoWell, addressing common questions patients might have about Type 2 diabetes, GlucoWell's potential side effects, and how GlucoWell can support their diabetes management journey. Maintain a clear, concise, and informative tone."

5. **Blog**:
    - **Prompt Example 1**:

      "Create a blog post for GlucoWell titled "Living Well with Type 2 Diabetes: Tips for Diet, Exercise, and Overall Health.' Offer practical advice and inspirational stories to empower patients and promote a holistic approach to diabetes management."
    - **Prompt Example 2**:

      "Develop a blog post titled 'Understanding Blood Sugar Levels: A Guide for Patients with Type 2 Diabetes." Explain blood sugar control, the importance of monitoring, and how GlucoWell can help.

Additional Tips:

- **Optimize for Search Engines**: Integrate relevant keywords throughout the website content to improve search engine ranking.
- **Patient Testimonials**: Include sections showcasing positive experiences and patient testimonials using GlucoWell's solutions.
- **Visual Appeal**: Utilize high-quality images and infographics to enhance user experience and break up text-heavy sections.
- **Mobile-Friendly Design**: Ensure the website is optimized for viewing on mobile devices, as many patients access health information through smartphones and tablets.

By tailoring these prompts to GlucoWell's specific brand identity and target audience, you can generate informative, engaging, and trustworthy website content that positions GlucoWell as a valuable resource for patients managing Type 2 diabetes.

7.2 Creating Targeted Advertising Copy with AI

The pharmaceutical industry relies heavily on targeted advertising to reach healthcare professionals (HCPs) and patients. However, crafting clear, compliant, and impactful messages can be challenging. Here's how AI, specifically prompt engineering, can be harnessed to develop targeted advertising copy for pharma companies.

Benefits of Using AI for Targeted Copy:

- **Personalization**: Create ad copy tailored to specific audience segments (e.g., HCP specialty, patient demographics, disease state).
- **Creative Efficiency**: Brainstorm a wider range of creative concepts quickly.
- **Data-Driven Insights**: Utilize patient data and market research to inform your prompts.
- **A/B Testing**: Generate multiple ad variations for A/B testing and optimize performance.

Examples of Prompt Engineering for Targeted Pharma Ads:

1. **HCP Audience (Targeted Display Ads):**
   - **Prompt Example:**

     "Develop a display ad copy for a new oncology medication targeting cardiologists. Highlight the medication's potential to reduce cardiovascular risks associated with traditional cancer treatments. Maintain a professional and data-driven tone, emphasizing clinical trial results."
2. **Patient Audience (Social Media Ads):**
   - **Prompt Example:**

     "Generate social media ad copy for a new medication managing migraine symptoms. Target adults aged 25-45 experiencing frequent migraines. Emphasize the medication's effectiveness in reducing migraine frequency and improving quality of life. Use an empathetic and helpful tone, with visuals depicting a pain-free, active lifestyle."

3. **Retargeting Campaigns**:
   - **Prompt Example**:

     "Create retargeting ad copy for a website offering an interactive tool for patients with chronic obstructive pulmonary disease (COPD). Target users who previously visited the website but did not sign up. Highlight the tool's benefits in managing symptoms and tracking progress. Offer a free trial or personalized recommendations as an incentive to return and explore the tool."

Challenges and Considerations:

- **Regulatory Compliance**: Ensure ad copy adheres to strict pharmaceutical advertising regulations regarding claims and disclaimers.
- **Human Oversight**: AI-generated content requires human review and editing to ensure accuracy, brand alignment, and ethical messaging.
- **Emotional Connection**: While AI can generate ideas, human creativity remains crucial for conveying empathy and emotional resonance in patient-facing ads.

How Pharma Uses Prompt Engineering:

Pharmaceutical Companies:

- Leverage AI to personalize display ads for HCPs based on their past interactions and areas of interest.
- Use AI to generate social media copy that targets specific patient demographics and disease states and highlights relevant treatment options.
- Employ to develop retargeting ad campaigns for patients who have previously interacted with their online resources,

encouraging them to engage further and learn more about specific medications.

Conclusion

Prompt engineering offers pharma companies a valuable tool to elevate their advertising efforts. By harnessing the power of AI to personalize content, generate creative ideas, and streamline workflows, pharma companies can reach their target audience with impactful messages that resonate and drive engagement. However, it's crucial to remember that AI serves as a support system, not a replacement for human expertise, regulatory compliance, and the importance of building trust with HCPs and patients.

7.3 Exercises: Develop Prompts to Write:

- **Website Content Sections for GlucoWell (e.g., FAQs, About us)**
- **Advertising Copy for GlucoWell Targeting Different Media (e.g., Print, Digital)**

Prompts for GlucoWell Website Content Sections:

1. **FAqs:**
   - **General Type 2 Diabetes**:
   - **Prompt Example 1**:
   - "Develop a series of FAQs addressing common questions about Type 2 diabetes, such as "What are the symptoms of Type 2 Diabetes?" Or "What causes Type 2 diabetes?" Maintain a clear, concise, and informative tone suitable for patients with a new diagnosis or limited disease knowledge."
   - **Prompt Example 2**:
   - "Craft FAQs from a patient newly diagnosed with Type 2 diabetes. Questions should include "How will I know if my treatment is working?" Or "What lifestyle changes can I make to manage my diabetes effectively?"
   - **GlucoWell Medication Specific**:
   - **Prompt Example**:
   - "Develop FAQs focused on GlucoWell's dosage forms. Address questions like 'How does GlucoWell work?' Or 'What are the potential side effects ofGlucoWell?' Ensure all information is medically accurate and disclaimers are included."
   - **Prompt Example**:

     "Craft FAQs related to the practicalities of using Glucowell. Questions could be 'How should I store GlucoWell?' Or 'Can I take GlucoWell with other medications?" Emphasize clear instructions and encourage patients to consult their doctor for personalized guidance."

2. **About Us:**
   - **Prompt Example 1:**
   - "Write a compelling 'About Us' page that tells GlucoWell's story. Highlight the company's mission, values, and what drives them to improve the lives of people with Type 2 diabetes. Briefly showcase the team's expertise and dedication to innovation in diabetes management solutions."
   - **Prompt Example 2**:
   - "Craft an 'About Us' page focusing on the science behind GlucoWell. Briefly explain its mechanism of action and the scientific research that led to its development. Maintain an informative tone while avoiding overly technical language."
3. **Additional Prompts:**
   - **Success Stories:**

     Prompt Example: "Develop a section showcasing real patient stories about their experience using GlucoWell. Highlight how GlucoWell has empowered them to manage their diabetes and live fulfilling lives."
   - **Blog**:
   - **Prompt Example 1**: "Create a blog post titled 'Healthy Living Tips for People with Type 2 Diabetes.' Offer practical advice on diet, exercise, stress management, and maintaining a positive outlook."
   - **Prompt Example 2**: "Develop a blog post titled "The Importance of Medication Adherence in Type 2 Diabetes Management.' Explain the benefits of taking medication as prescribed and offer strategies for overcoming adherence challenges."

Remember:

- Tailor the tone and complexity of the content to your target audience (newly diagnosed vs. experienced patients).

- Ensure all medical information is accurate and up-to-date.
- Maintain a consistent brand voice and message throughout the website.

7.4 Prompts for GlucoWell Advertising Copy (Print & Digital)

- **Target Audience**: People with Type 2 Diabetes (consider segmenting further by age and interests)
- **Overall Tone**: Empowering, informative, hopeful
- **Print Ads (Magazines, Doctor's Offce Brochures)**:
- **Headline Prompt**:
- "Write a captivating headline that grabs attention and sparks interest in GlucoWell.

Examples: "Take Control of Your Type 2 Diabetes, 'Live a Fuller Life with GlucoWell,' or 'Empowering You to Manage Your Blood Sugar."

- **Body Copy Prompt**:
- "Develop informative and concise body copy that explains how GluoWell helps manage Type 2 diabetes. Briefly mention the mechanism of action (without excessive technical jargon) and highlight key benefits like improved blood sugar control or simplified medication routine."
- **Call to Action Prompt**:
- "Craft a clear call to action encouraging readers to learn more about GlucoWell.

Examples: "Visit our website to discover how GlucoWell can help,' 'Talk to your doctor about GlucoWell today."

- **Visual Prompt**:
- "Consider the visuals that would best complement the ad copy. Think about using images of people living active lives or managing their diabetes with a sense of control."

Digital Ads (Social Media, Display Ads):

- **Headline Prompt**:
- "Develop short, engaging headlines for social ads or display banners".

Examples:

- Feeling Overwhelmed by Diabetes? GlucoWell can help,' or 'Don't Let Diabetes Slow You Down. Ask About GlucoWell."
- **Body Copy Prompt:**
- "Craft concise body copy that focuses on the emotional impact of managing Type 2 diabetes. Highlight how GlucoWell empowers patients and allows them to live more fulfilling lives. Consider using questions to spark engagement (e.g., "Ready to take control of your health?").
- **Call to Action Prompt:**
- "Create clear CTAs optimized for the digital platform. Examples: "Learn More now,' or 'Click Here to Find a Doctor Who Prescribes GlucoWell."
- **Targeting Prompt:**
- "Develop prompts to tailor your social media ad targeting. Consider demographics, interests related to diabetes management or online health communities."

Additional Considerations:

- **A/B Testing:** Utilize A/B testing to compare ad variations and optimize performance based on audience response.
- **Compliance:** Ensure all advertising copy adheres to pharmaceutical advertising regulations regarding claims and disclaimers.
- **Brand Consistency:** Maintain a consistent brand voice and message across all advertising materials (print and digital).

By tailoring these prompts to your target audience and media platform, you can generate compelling advertising copy that resonates with patients with Type 2 diabetes and encourages them to learn more about GlucoWell.

CHAPTER 8

Optimizing Your Prompts for Maximum Impact

In the competitive world of pharmaceutical marketing, crafting impactful and compliant messages is crucial. Here, we explore how prompt engineering can be leveraged to optimize your prompts for maximum impact in pharmaceutical content creation and advertising.

Optimizing Prompts: Key Strategies

1. **Target Audience Specificity**:
   - **Prompt Example**: "Develop social media posts for GlucoWell targeting patients newly diagnosed with Type 2 diabetes. Emphasize clear information about the disease and emotional support, using a reassuring and encouraging tone. Tailor posts for a younger audience (25-45) compared to an older audience (55+)."
2. **Desired Outcome Clarity**:
   - **Prompt Example**: "Generate website copy for GlucoWell. The goal is to educate healthcare professionals (HCPs) about the medication's clinical trial results and its potential benefits for patients. Maintain a professional, data-driven tone, highlighting key statistics and effcacy data."
3. **Emotional Nuance Integration**:
   - **Prompt Example**: "Create a script for a video testimonial featuring a patient using GlucoWell. Capture the emotions

associated with managing Type 2 diabetes, showcasing how GlucoWell has empowered the patient to live a more active and fulfilling life. Balance the emotional narrative with factual information about the medication's benefits."

4. **Brand Voice Consistency**:
   - **Prompt Example:** "Develop a series of blog posts on GlucoWell's website. While covering topics related to Type 2 diabetes management, ensure all posts maintain a consistent brand voice — informative, supportive, and empowering patients to take control of their health."

5. **Regulatory Compliance Adherence**:
   - **Prompt Example**: "Craft email marketing copy promoting a GlucoWell webinar for HCPs. Highlight the webinar's focus on the latest safety data for GlucoWell while ensuring all claims and disclaimers adhere to pharmaceutical advertising regulations."

Maximizing Impact: Additional Considerations

- **Leverage Data Insights**: Integrate patient data, market research, and industry trends into prompts to enhance content relevance and target specific needs.
- **A/B Testing**: Generate multiple prompt variations and test them to identify the most effective approach for your target audience and marketing goals.
- **Human-in-the-Loop Approach**: While AI is powerful, human oversight remains crucial. Utilize human expertise to refine prompts, ensure factual accuracy, and maintain brand alignment.

Conclusion

Prompt engineering offers a valuable tool for the pharmaceutical industry to optimize content creation and advertising efforts. By tailoring prompts to specific audiences, desired outcomes, and brand voice, pharma companies can craft impactful messages that resonate with patients and HCPs. However, it's essential to remember that AI serves as a support system, not a replacement for human creativity, medical expertise, and adherence to strict regulatory guidelines.

8.1 Fine-Tuning Prompts for Better Results

While prompt engineering is a powerful tool for creating pharmaceutical content, achieving optimal results often involves refinement, known as fine-tuning. This chapter explores strategies for fine-tuning prompts and maximizing their effectiveness in crafting impactful content for the pharmaceutical industry.

The Importance of Fine-Tuning Prompts:

- **Improved Accuracy:** Fine-tuning helps ensure that AI-generated information aligns with medical realities and adheres to scientific principles.
- **Enhanced Relevance:** Refining prompts allow you to tailor content to specific audiences (HCPs vs. patients) and address their unique needs and interests.
- **Brand Voice Consistency:** Fine-tuning helps maintain a consistent brand voice and messaging across all communications, fostering trust and brand recognition.
- **Regulatory Compliance:** Precise, prompt crafting minimizes the risk of generating content that violates pharmaceutical advertising regulations.

Fine-Tuning Strategies for Pharma Content:

1. **Iterative Feedback Loop:**
   - **Prompt Example:**

     "Develop the initial draft of a blog post for GlucoWell on managing stress and its impact on blood sugar levels in Type 2 diabetes. Use feedback from subject matter experts (SMEs) like endocrinologists or patient educators to refine the content's accuracy, clarity, and adherence to best practices."
2. **A/B Testing for Optimization:**
   - **Prompt Example:**
   - "Generate two variations of social media ad copy for GlucoWell, targeting patients with Type 2 diabetes experiencing frequent fatigue. A/B test both versions to

determine which ad resonates better with the target audience and drives higher engagement."

3. **Leveraging Domain-Specific Data**:
    - **Prompt Example**:
    - "Fine-tune prompts for GlucoWell's website content by incorporating anonymized patient data on common challenges and concerns related to Type 2 diabetes management. This data can help tailor content to address real-world patient experiences."
4. **Utilizing Pre-Trained Pharmacological Models**:
    - **Prompt Example**:
    - Many large language models are pre-trained on vast scientific and medical text data. Utilize these models as a starting point for fine-tuning prompts specific to the pharmaceutical domain.

Additional Considerations:

- **Human Expertise Remains Crucial**: AI-generated content requires human review and editing to ensure factual accuracy, brand alignment, and ethical messaging.
- **Start Small and Scale Gradually**. Fine-tune prompts for specific content pieces and gradually expand as you gain experience and confidence.
- **Track and Analyze Results**: Monitor the performance of your content and use the insights to refine your fine-tuning approach further.

Conclusion

Fine-tuning prompts is an ongoing process that ensures your AI-generated content delivers the desired impact within the pharmaceutical industry. By continuously refining, leveraging expert feedback, and utilizing data-driven insights, you can optimize your content to resonate with target audiences, adhere to regulations, and serve the healthcare community.

8.2 Evaluation Metrics: Measuring the Success of Your Prompts

In pharma marketing, evaluating the effectiveness of your content creation methods is crucial. When it comes to prompt engineering, specific metrics can help you assess the success of your prompts and identify areas for improvement.

Metrics for Evaluating Prompts in Pharma Marketing:

1. **Content Quality and Accuracy**:
   - **Metric Example— Subject Matter Expert (SME) Review**: Have healthcare professionals (doctors, pharmacists) reviewed the content generated by your prompts? Do they find it medically accurate, informative, and up-to-date?
   - **Metric Example— Fact-Checking Process**: Is there a rigorous fact-checking process to ensure the factual accuracy of all content generated using your prompts?
2. **Audience Engagement**:
   - **Metric Example — Website Traffic & User Behavior:** Do your prompts increase website traffc and user engagement with your content (e.g., time spent on pages, downloads of resources)?
   - **Metric Example — Social Media Interactions:** Are your pharma brand's prompts generating social media engagement (likes, comments, shares)? Are they generating content?
3. **Brand Alignment and Tone**:
   - **Metric Example — Brand Consistency Review:** Does the content generated by your prompts align with your brand voice, messaging, and overall brand identity?
   - **Metric Example - Target Audience Pereiption Surveys:** Have you conducted surveys to gauge how your target audience perceives the tone and message in content generated using your prompts?

4. **Campaign Performance (if applicable)**:
    - **Metric Example – HCP Awareness & Lead Generation:** Do your prompts increase awareness of your brand among HCPs and generate qualified leads for your sales team?
    - **Metric Example – Patient Education & Activation:** Do your prompts effectively educate patients about their condition and empower them to manage their health actively?
    - **Metric Example – Regulatory Compliance:** Have there been any non-compliance issues with pharmaceutical advertising regulations due to content generated by prompts?

Additional Considerations:

- **Multi-Metric Approach:** Use a combination of metrics to understand your prompts' impact better. Don't rely solely on a single metric.
- **Benchmarking**: Benchmark your metrics against industry standards or internal goals to assess progress and identify areas for improvement.
- **Long-Term Evaluation**: Evaluating the success of prompts is an ongoing process. Monitor metrics continuously and adapt your approach based on the data you gather.

Conclusion

By measuring the success of your prompts through relevant metrics, you can ensure they generate high-quality, impactful content that resonates with your target audience and aligns with your brand identity in the pharmaceutical industry. Remember, AI-generated content requires human oversight and continuous evaluation to optimize its effectiveness and ensure compliance with industry regulations.

8.3 The Future of Prompt Engineering in Pharma Marketing

Prompt engineering is rapidly evolving, and its potential applications in pharmaceutical marketing continue to expand. This section explores exciting future trends that promise to revolutionize how pharmaceutical companies develop and deliver marketing messages.

Emerging Trends in Pharma Prompt Engineering:

1. **Personalized Patient Education**:
   - **Example**: Consider prompts that generate personalized medication adherence reminders for patients, considering their preferences and challenges.
2. **Interactive Chatbots for Patient Support**:
   - **Example**: Develop prompts to fine-tune a chatbot that provides real-time AI-powered support to patients managing chronic conditions, addressing their specific concerns, and offering tailored resources.
3. **Generating Compelling Patient Testimonials**:
   - **Example**: Utilize prompts to craft realistic and impactful patient testimonials that showcase the positive experiences of using a specific medication while adhering to ethical considerations.
4. **AI-Powered Content Personalization Across Channels**:
   - **Example**: Imagine prompts that adapt website content, email marketing messages, and social media posts to individual HCP or patient profiles, delivering highly relevant targeted information.
5. **Optimizing Content for Voice Search**:
   - **Example**: Develop prompts to generate content specifically optimized for voice search queries, ensuring patients can easily find answers to their health questions using voice assistants.

Future Applications:

In the future, pharmaceutical companies:

- Could leverage prompts to create personalized medication management plans for patients with heart disease, incorporating factors like lifestyle and medication adherence.
- Might utilize AI-powered chatbots with prompts fine-tuned to address specific concerns of allergy patients, offering real-time guidance and support.
- Could explore prompts to generate patient testimonials in various formats (video, text) that resonate with different demographics and effectively communicate the benefits of their oncology treatments.

Challenges and Considerations for the Future:

- **Ethical Considerations**: Ensure AI-generated content adheres to ethical principles, avoids bias, and prioritizes patient well-being.
- **Regulatory Landscape**: As AI evolves, staying abreast of changing regulations and maintaining compliance will be crucial.
- **A human-in-the-loop Approach**: While AI has immense potential, human expertise remains vital for oversight, creative direction, and brand alignment.

Conclusion

Prompt engineering offers a powerful tool for pharma marketing, and its future holds immense promise. By embracing these emerging trends and navigating potential challenges, pharmaceutical companies can leverage AI to create impactful, personalized, and compliant content that empowers patients, educates HCPs, and improves healthcare outcomes. Remember, AI is a valuable collaborator, not a replacement for human creativity, medical expertise, and ethical responsibility in pharmaceutical marketing.

Part IV. Conclusion

9. The Future of Pharma Branding: A World Powered by AI and Human Creativity

10. Measuring the Success of Prompts in Pharma Marketing

11. The Future of Prompt Engineering in Pharmaceutical Marketing: Emerging Trends

CHAPTER

9

The Future of Pharma Branding: A World Powered by AI and Human Creativity

The pharmaceutical industry is on the cusp of a branding revolution. Artificial Intelligence (AI), specifically prompt engineering, offers a powerful tool to craft compelling and impactful brand experiences for patients and healthcare professionals (HCPs). However, the key to success lies in a harmonious blend of AI's efficiency and human creativity. This chapter explores how pharmaceutical companies can leverage this dynamic duo to shape the future of their brands.

The Power of AI in Pharma Branding:

- **Personalized Patient Experiences**: AI can personalize brand messaging based on patient demographics, disease states, and treatment journeys. Imagine a brand that delivers targeted educational resources and support programs, fostering a sense of connection and care. For example, a diabetes medication brand utilizes AI to create personalized social media campaigns that offer recipe suggestions and exercise tips tailored to individual patient needs.
- **Data-Driven Brand Insights**: AI can analyze vast healthcare data to identify patient attitudes, perceptions, and unmet needs. This allows brands to tailor their messaging and offerings to resonate deeply with target audiences. For instance, an oncology treatment brand leverages AI to analyze patient support group discussions, uncovering concerns about hair loss. The brand then develops a targeted campaign highlighting treatment options with minimal hair loss side effects.

- **Empowering Storytelling**: AI can help craft compelling patient stories that showcase a brand's real-life impact. This fosters trust and an emotional connection with potential patients. For example, an AI-powered platform helps generate video testimonials for a rare disease treatment. Patients share their journeys, struggles, and triumphs, offering hope and inspiration to others facing similar challenges.

The Irreplaceable Role of Human Creativity

- **Emotional Intelligence:** AI excels at processing data, but human creativity adds the layer of emotional intelligence crucial for branding success. Humans understand empathy. For example, a brand's creative team refines an AI-generated patient testimonial script, infusing it with warmth and humor to ensure it resonates with viewers on a deeper level.
- **Strategic Vision**: Humans set the strategic direction for the brand, ensuring AI-generated content aligns with brand values, mission, and long-term goals. For instance, a brand's leadership team establishes a brand identity prioritizing patient empowerment. They guide AI prompts to generate content that reflects this value, such as educational resources focused on self-management and healthy lifestyle choices.
- **Ethical Considerations**: Humans ensure that AI-generated content adheres to ethical principles. These include avoiding bias, respecting patient privacy, and promoting responsible healthcare practices. For example, a brand's marketing team carefully reviews AI-generated social media ad copy to ensure that it accurately represents the medication's benefits and potential side effects and avoids misleading information.

The Future of Pharma Branding: A Collaborative Approach

- **Human-in-the-Loop Process**: The most successful brand strategies leverage AI as a powerful collaborator, not a replacement for human expertise. Humans set the direction, provide oversight, and inject the emotional intelligence that resonates with audiences.

- **Iterative Refinement**: Brand messaging and content should be continuously refined based on performance metrics and feedback from patients and HCPs.
- **Evolving Technologies**: As AI capabilities expand, new opportunities for crafting even more personalized and impactful brand experiences will emerge.

Future Applications of Pharma Companies:

- Could utilize AI to develop interactive patient communities focused on specific disease areas. Patients can share experiences, offer encouragement, and access brand-sponsored educational resources, all within a safe and supportive environment.
- Might leverage AI to generate personalized medication adherence reminders that incorporate not just dosage information but also motivational messages and tips for integrating medication into daily routines.

We could explore AI-powered chatbots that provide real-time patient support and answer questions about their medications and potential side effects, creating a brand identity focused on patient well-being and accessibility.

Conclusion

The future of pharma branding lies in a powerful collaboration between AI and human creativity. By leveraging both strengths, pharmaceutical companies can create patient-centric brands that deliver personalized experiences, build trust, and improve health outcomes. The journey ahead promises exciting possibilities for shaping a new era of pharma branding driven by innovation, empathy, and a commitment to serving patients' needs.

9.1 The Ethical Considerations of Prompt Engineering in Pharma

Prompt engineering offers a powerful tool for pharma marketing, but its use requires careful consideration of ethical implications. This section explores the key ethical concerns surrounding prompt engineering in pharmaceutical marketing.

1. **Bias and Fairness:**
   - **Challenge**: AI algorithms can perpetuate existing biases in healthcare data, leading to content that unfairly targets certain demographics or glosses over potential side effects for specific patient groups.
   - **Mitigation Strategies**:
     - Employ diverse datasets for training AI models.
     - Utilize fairness metrics to identify and address bias in generated content.
     - Ensure prompts are inclusive and avoid language that reinforces stereotypes.

2. **Transparency and Explainability**:
   - **Challenge**: Understanding how AI models arrive at specific content generated through prompts can be difficult. This lack of transparency can raise concerns about the accuracy and trustworthiness of the information.
   - **Mitigation Strategies**:
     - Maintain clear documentation of the prompts used for content generation.
     - Utilize interpretable AI models that provide insights into the reasoning behind generated content.
     - Ensure clear disclaimers are displayed alongside AI-generated content.

3. **Privacy and Data Protection**:
   - **Challenge**: Content generation may involve using patient data and raising concerns about privacy and confidentiality.

- **Mitigation Strategies**:
  - Anonymize patient data used for training AI models.
  - Implement robust data security measures.
  - Obtain clear patient consent for data usage in content generation.

4. **Misinformation and Deception**:
   - **Challenge**: AI-generated content could be misleading or inaccurate, potentially harming patients or creating unrealistic expectations about treatment outcomes.
   - **Mitigation Strategies**:
     - Subject all AI-generated content to rigorous fact-checking by medical professionals.
     - Ensure prompts are clear and specific to avoid ambiguity in the generated content.
     - Prioritize scientific accuracy and avoid sensationalized language.
5. **Over-Reliance on AI and Dehumanization of Healthcare**:
   - **Challenge**: Overdependence on AI for content generation could lead to a disconnect with patients and a disregard for the human element of healthcare.
   - **Mitigation Strategies**:
     - Maintain a human-in-the-loop approach where human expertise guides and oversees AI-generated content.
     - Ensure content emphasizes empathy and patient well-being.
     - Prioritize clear communication channels for patients to interact with healthcare professionals.

Conclusion

Prompt engineering in pharmaceutical marketing holds immense potential, but ethical considerations must be prioritized. By actively addressing bias, ensuring transparency, protecting data privacy and maintaining a human-centric approach, pharmaceutical companies can leverage AI responsibly to create impactful, ethical, and trustworthy content that efficiently serves patients and healthcare professionals.

9.2 The Human - AI Partnership: The Future of Successful Pharma Branding

The landscape of pharmaceutical branding is undergoing a significant shift. Artificial intelligence (AI), specifically prompt engineering, offers a powerful tool for personalizing patient experiences, crafting compelling brand narratives, and improving health outcomes. However, the key to success lies in a harmonious partnership between human creativity and AI's efficiency. Here's how this dynamic duo will shape the future of pharmaceutical branding.

The Strengths of AI in Pharma Branding:

- **Personalization**: AI analyzes data and tailors brand messaging to specific patient demographics, disease states, and treatment journeys. Imagine a brand that delivers targeted education resources and support programs, fostering a deep connection with each patient.
- **Data-Driven Insights**: AI can analyze vast healthcare data to identify patient attitudes, perceptions, and unmet needs. This allows brands to refine their messaging and offerings to resonate with target audiences more deeply.
- **Content Creation Eûciency**: AI can quickly and efficiently generate different content formats (website copy, social media posts, video scripts), allowing brands to adapt their communication strategies more readily.

The Irreplaceable Role of Human Creativity:

- **Emotional Intelligence**: While AI excels at processing data, human creativity injects the essential layer of emotional intelligence for brand success. Human empathy, trust, and hope — are crucial for building strong brand connections with patients.

- **Strategic Vision**: Humans set the strategic direction for the brand, ensuring AI-generated content aligns with brand values, mission, and long-term goals. Creative teams translate brand strategy into clear prompts for AI, guiding the content creation process.
- **Ethical Considerations**: Humans ensure that AI-generated content adheres to ethical principles. These include avoiding bias, respecting patient privacy, and promoting responsible healthcare practices.

The Future of Pharma Branding: A Collaborative Approach

- **Human-in-the-Loop Process**: The most successful branding strategies leverage AI is a powerful collaborator, not a replacement for human expertise. Humans set the direction, provide oversight, and infuse the emotional intelligence that resonates with audiences.
- **Iterative Refinement**: Brand messaging and content should be continuously refined based on performance metrics and feedback from patients and HCPs (Healthcare professionals).
- **Evolving Technologies**: As AI capabilities expand, new opportunities for crafting even more personalized and impactful brand experiences will emerge.

Examples of Human Partnership in Action:

- **Scenario**: A diabetes medication brand aims to create a social media campaign that resonates with young adults newly diagnosed with Type 1 diabetes.
- **Human Role**: The brand's marketing team develops a campaign strategy focused on empowerment and managing diabetes alongside an active lifestyle. They create prompts for AI that capture this tone and target specific demographics.

- **AI Role**: AI generates social media posts featuring inspirational stories from young adults with Type 1 diabetes and tips for managing the condition while staying active and engaged.

Benefits of the Collaboration:

- The campaign resonates with the target audience due to AI's data-driven personalization and human-crafted emotional connection.
- The brand is a trusted partner for young adults navigating Type 1 diabetes.

Conclusion

The future of pharmaceutical branding belongs to the powerful partnership between human creativity and AI. By harnessing both strengths, pharmaceutical companies can create patient-centric brands that deliver personalized experiences, build trust, and improve healthcare outcomes. This journey promises exciting possibilities for shaping a new era of pharmaceutical branding driven by innovation, empathy, and a commitment to serving patients' needs responsibly and ethically.

CHAPTER 10

Measuring the Success of Prompts in Pharma Marketing

Evaluating the effectiveness of your content creation methods is crucial in pharmaceutical marketing. When it comes to prompt engineering, specific metrics can help you assess the success of your prompts and identify areas for improvement.

Metrics for Evaluating Prompts in Pharma Marketing:

1. **Content Quality and Accuracy**:
   - **Subject Matter Expert (SME) Review**: Have Healthcare professionals (doctors, pharmacists) reviewed the content generated by your prompts? Do they find it medically accurate, informative, and up-to-date?
   - **Fact-Checking Process**: Is there a rigorous fact-checking process in place to ensure the factual accuracy of all content generated using your prompts?
2. **Audience Engagement**:
   - **Website Traffic & User Behavior**: Do your prompts increase website traffic and user engagement with your content (e.g., time spent on pages and resource downloads)?
   - **Social Media Interactions**: Are your prompts generating social media engagement (likes, comments, shares) for your pharma brand's content?

3. **Brand Alignment and Tone**:
    - **Brand Consistency Review**: Does the content generated by your prompts align with your brand voice, messaging, and overall brand identity?
    - **Target Audience Perception Surveys**: Have you conducted surveys to gauge how your target audience perceives the tone and message conveyed in content generated using your prompts?
4. **Campaign Performance (If applicable)**:
    - **HCP Awareness & Lead Generation**: Are your prompts leading to increased awareness of your brand among HCPs and generating qualified leads for your sales team?
    - **Patient Education & Activation**: Do your prompts effectively educate patients about their condition and empower them to manage their health actively.
    - **Regulatory Compliance**: Have there been any non-compliance issues with pharmaceutical advertising regulations due to content generated by your prompts?

Examples: Some of the leading pharmaceutical companies.

- Track website traffic and user behavior to determine which content generated by prompts resonate most with HCPs, informing future prompt refinement. Measure social media engagement metrics to identify the most effective prompts for creating patient-facing content that sparks conversations and drives brand awareness.
- Conduct brand consistency reviews to ensure content generated by prompts aligns with their patient-centric brand voice and avoids any potential messaging misalignment.

Additional Considerations:

- **Multi-Metric Approach**: Use a combination of metrics to understand your prompts' impact better. Don't rely solely on a single metric.

- **Benchmarking**: Benchmark your metrics against industry standards or internal goals to assess progress and identify areas for improvement.
- **Long-Term Evaluation**: Evaluating the success of prompts is an ongoing process. Monitor metrics continuously and adapt your approach based on the data you gather.

Conclusion

By measuring the success of your prompts through relevant metrics, you can ensure they generate high-quality, impactful content that resonates with your target audience and aligns with your brand identity in the pharmaceutical industry. Remember, AI-generated content requires human oversight and continuous evaluation to optimize its effectiveness and ensure compliance with industry regulations.

CHAPTER 11

The Future of Prompt Engineering in Pharmaceutical Marketing: Emerging Trends

Prompt engineering is rapidly evolving, and its potential applications in pharmaceutical marketing continue to expand. Here, we explore some exciting future trends that promise to revolutionize how pharmaceutical companies develop and deliver marketing messages.

Emerging Trends in Prompt Engineering in Pharma:

1. **Personalized Patient Education**:
    - **Example**: Imagine prompts that generate personalized medication adherence reminders for patients, considering their preferences and challenges.
2. **Interactive Chatbots for Patient Support**:
    - **Example**: Develop prompts to fine-tune a chatbot that provides real-time AI-powered support to patients managing chronic conditions, addressing their specific concerns, and offering tailored resources.
3. **Generating Compelling Patient Testimonials**:
    - **Example**: Utilize prompts to craft realistic and impactful patient testimonials that showcase the positive experiences of using a specific medication while adhering to to ethical considerations.

4. **AI-Powered Content Personalization Across Channels**:
    - **Example**: Imagine prompts that adapt website content, email marketing messages, and social media posts to individual HCPs or patient profiles, delivering highly relevant and targeted information.
5. **Optimizing Content for Voice Search**:
    - **Example**: Develop prompts to generate content optimized for voice search queries. This will ensure that patients can easily find answers to their health questions using voice assistants.

Examples of Future Applications:

Pharmaceutical companies can:

- Leverage prompts to create personalized medication management plans for patients with heart disease. These plans should incorporate factors like lifestyle and medication adherence.
- Pharma companies utilize AI-powered chatbots with prompts fine-tuned to address specific concerns of allergy patients, offering real-time guidance and support. Explore prompts to generate patient testimonials in various formats (video, text) that resonate with different demographics and effectively communicate the benefits of their oncology treatment.

Challenges and Considerations for the Future:

- **Ethical Considerations**: Ensure AI-generated content adheres to ethical principles, avoids bias, and prioritizes patient well-being.
- **Regulatory Landscape**: As AI evolves, staying abreast of changing regulations and maintaining compliance will be crucial.
- **A Human-in-the-loop Approach**: While AI has immense potential, human expertise remains vital for oversight, creative direction, and brand alignment.

Conclusion

Prompt engineering offers a powerful tool for pharmaceutical marketing, and its future holds immense promise. By embracing these emerging trends and navigating potential challenges, pharmaceutical companies can leverage AI to create impactful, personalized, and compliant content that empowers patients, educates HCPs, and improves healthcare outcomes. Remember, AI is a valuable collaborator, not a replacement for human creativity, medical expertise, and ethical responsibility in pharmaceutical marketing.

Conclusion

In conclusion, prompt engineering represents a transformative force in pharmaceutical marketing. By harnessing the power of AI to tailor prompts, pharmaceutical companies can create high-quality, targeted content that resonates with specific audiences, adheres to strict regulations, and serves the healthcare community.

This approach offers numerous benefits, from personalizing patient education to optimizing content for diûerent channels. As AI technology evolves, we can expect even more exciting applications of prompt engineering in pharma marketing. However, it's crucial to remember that AI serves as a support system, not a replacement for human expertise, ethical considerations, and the importance of building trust with patients and HCPs.

By adopting a human-in-the-loop approach, leveraging data-driven insights, and continuously evaluating the effectiveness of prompts, pharma companies can unlock this technology's full potential and revolutionize how they connect with their target audiences. The future of pharma marketing lies in leveraging the power of AI to deliver impactful, personalized, and compliant messages that empower patients, educate HCPs, and improve health outcomes.

Appendix

1. Examples of Prompts for Pharma Brand Management
2. Glossary
3. Resources for Further Learning on Prompt Engineering

Examples of Prompts for Pharma Brand Management

The section presents ten prompts illustrating how prompt engineering can be used in pharmaceutical brand management.

1. Prompts for Creating the Name for a Pharma Brand
2. Prompts for Crafting a Meaningful Positioning Statement for Your Pharma Brand
3. Prompts for Crafting a Pharma Brand Identity
4. Prompts for Identifying Points of Parity and Points of Differentiation for Your Pharma Brand
5. Prompts for Managing the Lifecycle of a Pharmaceutical Brand
6. Prompts for Customer Journey Mapping for a Pharma Brand
7. Prompts for Personalizing Communication for All Types of Customers (HCPs, Patients, Payers, Regulators, and Investors)
8. Prompts for Creating a Chatbot for Patient Support
9. Prompts for Creating Healthy Lunch Options for a Diabetic Patient
10. Prompts for Creating a Multi-Dimensional Value Proposition for Payers

1. Prompts for Creating the Name for a Pharma Brand

1. **Target Audience & Conditions**:
   - Who is this medication for? (Age group, specific conditions, demographics.)
   - What emotions do you want the brand name to evoke in patients? (Hope, strength, empowerment, etc.)
2. **Brand Positioning & Benefits**:
   - What is the medication's unique selling proposition (USP)? (Innovation, speed of action, fewer side effects)
   - What are the key benefits of the medication? (Improved quality of life, symptom relief, disease management)
3. **Brand Name Characteristics**:
   - Should the name be descriptive or evocative? (Descriptive - reveals the condition or action; Evocative -creates a feeling).
   - What is the desired length and pronunciation of the name? (Short, memorable, easy to pronounce)
   - Does the name sound scientific, modern, or natural? (Consider the brand image you want to convey)
4. **Practical Considerations**:
   - Is the name available as a trademark and domain name? (Crucial to avoid legal issues)
   - Can the name be easily spelled and remembered? (Important for patients and HCPs to recall)
   - Does the name have any negative connotations in different languages? (Global considerations)
5. **Creative Prompts**:
   - Use Latin or Greek roots related to the condition or mechanism of action.
   - Combine existing words to create a new, unique name.
   - Use a metaphor or analogy to represent the medication's effect.

- Invent a completely new word that sounds scientific and memorable.

Some Examples of Prompts:

Here are some prompts to guide you in brainstorming brand names for a pharmaceutical brand, categorized by different approaches:

A. **Benefit-Oriented Prompts**:

- Focus on the key benefit or outcome your medication provides.
- **Prompt:** "Generate names that evoke feelings of [desired feeling] associated with the medication's benefit (e.g., energy, relief, clarity)."
- Highlight the mechanism of action (MOA) of the medication creatively.
- **Prompt:** "Craft names that metaphorically capture how the medication works *within the body*."

B. **Target Audience-Oriented Prompts**:

- Consider the specific needs and demographics of your target patient population.
- **Prompt:** "Generate names that resonate with [patient age group] struggling with [condition]."
- Evoke a sense of empowerment or hope for patients.
- **Prompt:** "Develop names that convey a feeling of [desired emotion] for patients managing their health."

C. **Brand Identity-Oriented Prompts**:

- Capture the core values and personality you want your brand to embody.
- **Prompt:** "Create names that reflect our brand's commitment to [core value] and [core value]."
- Evoke a sense of trust and reliability.
- **Prompt:** "Generate names that convey a feeling of [desired feeling] associated with our brand's reputation."

D. **Creative Prompts**:

- Utilize alliteration or rhyme for a memorable name.

- **Prompt:** "Develop names that use alliteration or rhyme to enhance recall."
- Employ wordplay or metaphors related to the medication or condition.
- **Prompt:** "Craft names incorporating clever wordplay or metaphors related to [medication/condition]."

E. **Practical Prompts**:

- Ensure the name is easy to pronounce, spell, and remember.
- **Prompt:** "Generate names that are short, pronounceable, and easy to spell."
- Check for trademark availability before finalizing a name.
- **Prompt:** "After brainstorming a shortlist, research trademark availability to ensure a clear path forward."

F. **Additional Prompt**:

- Combine elements from different categories to create a unique and impactful brand name.
- **Prompt:** "Develop names that combine a benefit-oriented term with a creative wordplay element, reflecting our brand's commitment to innovation."

Remember:

- Tailor the prompts to your specific medication and target audience.
- Brainstorm many names to increase your chances of finding the perfect one.
- Get feedback from colleagues and potential patients to refine your final selection.

You can generate a compelling name for your pharma brand by utilizing these prompts and following these steps.

2. Prompts for Crafting a Meaningful Positioning Statement for Your Pharma Brand

A. Target Audience and Needs:

- Who is this medication for? (Age group, specific conditions, demographics)
- What are the biggest challenges your target audience facing currently? (Physical, emotional, social).
- What the the patient's unmet needs or desires related to their condition?

(Improved symptom control, fewer side effects, increased convenience).

B. Brand Benefits & Diûerentiation:

- What is the medication's unique selling proposition (USP)? (Innovation, mechanism of action, superior efficacy).
- How does your brand address the patient's unmet needs better than competitors?

  (Faster relief, reduced dosing frequency, improved tolerability).
- What are the key emotional benefits patients experience with your medication?

  (Hope, empowerment, regaining control of their life).

C. Positioning Statement Structure:

- **Who**: Identify the target audience (e.g., Adults with chronic migraines..)
- **Problem**: Briefly state the patient's challenge (e.g., experiencing debilitating headaches...)
- **Solution:** Highlight your brand's unique benefit (e.g., [Brand Name] provides fast-acting relief...)
- **Outcome:** Describe the positive result for patients (e.g., Allowing them to return to their day quickly.)

D. Additional Prompts:

- What scientific evidence supports the brand's claims? (Include relevant data in the positioning statement if appropriate)

- What is the brand's overall value proposition? (Beyond symptom relief, how does it improve patients' lives?)
- What emotional connection do you want to establish with your patients? (Consider using language that evokes hope, confidence, or empowerment.)

Addressing these prompts can help you craft a compelling and meaningful positioning statement that communicates the value your pharmaceutical brand offers patients. Remember, the positioning statement should be concise and memorable and differentiate your brand from competitors.

3. Prompts for Crafting a Pharma Brand Identity

Here are some prompts to guide you in developing a strong brand identity for your pharma brand, categorized by key aspects:

1. **Core Values and Mission**:
   - **Mission: Prompt:** "What is our brand's fundamental purpose in improving patient lives?"
   - **Values**: **Prompt:** "Identify 3 to 5 core values that define our brand's character and guide our actions. (e.g., Innovation, patient-centricity, trust)."
2. **Target Audience**:
   - **Patient Profile**: **Prompt:** "Describe the typical patient we aim to serve in detail (age, demographics, condition, needs, aspirations)."
   - **HCP (Healthcare Professional) Perspective: Prompt:** "How do we want HCPs *to* perceive our brand and medication compared to competitors?"
3. **Brand Personality**:
   - **Brand Voice**: **Prompt:** "If our brand were a person, how would it communicate? (e.g., empathetic, authoritative, informative, approachable)."
   - **Emotional Connection**: **Prompt:**"What emotions do we want patients to associate with our brand (e.g., hope, empowerment, trust, well-being)?"
4. **Visual Identity**:
   - **Color Palette**: **Prompt:** "What emotions and values do we want our brand colors to convey (e.g., blue for trust, green for growth, yellow for optimism)?"
   - **Logo Design**: **Prompt:** "Craft a simple, memorable logo that visually represents our brand identity."
5. **Brand Messaging**:
   - **Benefit Highlighting**: **Prompt:** "How can we communicate the key benefits and the value proposition of our medication clearly and concisely?"

- **Differentiation Strategy**: **Prompt:** "What unique selling proposition (USP) sets our brand apart from competitors? How can we leverage it in messaging?"

Additional Prompts:

- **Brand Story**: **Prompt:**"Develop a compelling brand story that resonates with patients and conveys our passion for improving health outcomes?"
- **Customer Experience**: **Prompt:**"How can we create a seamless and positive patient experience at every touchpoint with our brand?"

Remember:

- Tailor the prompts to your specific medication and target audience.
- Conduct market research to understand patient needs and competitor strategies.
- Ensure all aspects of your brand identity (messaging, visuals, customer experience) work cohesively to create a unified brand image.

By brainstorming and refining answers to these prompts, you will be well on your way to establish a strong and memorable brand identity that connects with patients and healthcare professionals alike.

4. Prompts for Identifying Points of Parity and Points of Differentiation for Your Pharma Brand

Understanding the Competitive Landscape:

- Who are your main competitors in the market? (Identify brands with similar medications or targeting the same conditions)
- What are the standard features and benefits offered by competitors? (Effcacy, dosage forms, side effects, administration methods)
- What are the current industry trends and regulations? (Focus on specific patient populations, advancements in delivery systems, safety considerations)

Identifying Points of Parity (POP):

- What features and benefits does your brand share with competitors? (Mechanism of action, treatment area, basic efficacy)
- What essential elements do patients and HCPs expect from any medication in this category? (Safety, efficacy, affordability)
- What are the regulatory requirements that all brands must meet? (Safety trials, approval processes, labeling information)

Identifying Points of Differentiation (POD):

- What unique features and benefits set your brand apart from competitors? (Novel mechanism of action, superior efficacy, fewer side effects, innovative delivery method)
- What specific patient needs are not currently being met by existing brands? (Improved adherence options, reduced dosing frequency, better tolerability in specific populations)
- Does your brand have a compelling clinical advantage supported by strong scientific data? (Head-to-head trials, improved patient outcomes)

Additional Prompts:

- How can you leverage your brand's scientific heritage or research and development strengths?

- Does your brand offer any unique patient support programs or additional services? (Adherence reminders, educational materials, personalized treatment plans)
- Can you differentiate your brand through a more efficient manufacturing process or cost-effectiveness?

You can understand your brand's market position by systematically analyzing these prompts. Focusing on your unique selling points (PODs) will allow you to create a targeted marketing strategy that resonates with patients and healthcare professionals, leading to brand preference and market success.

Identifying Points of Parity (POPs) and Points of Difference (PODs):

Examples of Prompts

1. **Competitive Analysis Prompts:**
    - **Prompt**: "List 3 to 5 competitors for our medication (brand name). Identify each competitor's key features, benefits, and marketing messages."
    - **Response**:

1. Metformin
2. Januvia (Sitagliptin)
3. Victoza (Liraglutide)
4. Jardiance (Empagliflozin)
    - What common features and benefits do our medication and its main competitors share? These are our key points of parity."
    - "What are our medication's unique features and benefits that differentiate it from competitors?" These are our potential Points of Difference.
    - "How do our competitors position themselves in the market? What are their key messages and target audiences?"

2. **Product Attribute Prompts**:
   - "List all the key features and attributes of our medication (e.g., mechanism of action, dosage, side effects profile, duration of therapy)."
   - "Which features are considered standard or expected within this therapeutic class (Points of Parity)."
   - "Which features are unique or superior to our competitors (Points of Difference)?"
   - "How can we translate these unique features into meaningful patient benefits?"
3. **Patient Needs and Preferences Prompts**:
   - "What are the unmet needs and frustrations of patients currently using existing therapies for this condition?"
   - "How does our medication address these unmet needs better than competitors?"
   - "What are our target patient population's key priorities and concerns?"
   - "How can we position our medication to address these priorities and alleviate patient concerns?"
4. **Brand Value Prompts**:
   - "How do our brand values (e.g., innovation, patient-centricity, quality) translate into unique product features or benefits?"
   - "How can we communicate these brand values through our positioning and messaging?"
5. **SWOT Analysis Prompts:**
   - "Conduct a SWOT analysis of our medication. Identify our Strengths, Weaknesses, Opportunities, and Threats."
   - "How can we leverage our *Strengths* and *Opportunities* to differentiate our medication?"
   - How can we mitigate our *Weaknesses* and *Threats* to maintain a competitive advantage?"

Remember:

- Continuously refine your analysis and adjust your positioning as needed.
- Conduct market research and gather patient feedback to validate your assumptions.
- Communicate your positioning statement clearly and consistently across all marketing channels.

By effectively identifying and communicating your *Points of Parity* and *Points of Difference*, you can establish a strong competitive advantage and build a successful brand in the pharmaceutical market.

5. Prompts for Managing the Lifecycle of a Pharmaceutical Brand

1. Pre-Launch Phase

A. Market Research:

- What unmet needs exist in the target therapeutic area?
- Who are the key competitors, and how will your brand differentiate?
- What is the target patient population and their decision-making process?

B. Brand Development:

- Define the brand identity, personality, and core values.
- Craft a meaningful positioning statement and brand messaging.
- Develop a distinctive brand name and visual identity (logo, colors)

C. Regulatory Approval Strategy:

- Plan clinical trials and gather data to support safety and efficacy claims.
- Develop a robust regulatory filing strategy to obtain marketing authorization.

2. Launch Phase

A. Marketing & Sales Strategy:

- Identify the most effective channels to reach healthcare professionals (HCPs) and patients.
- Develop targeted marketing campaigns to educate HCPs and raise awareness among patients.
- Establish a strong sales force to promote the brand and secure prescriptions.

B. Patient Access & Reimbursement:

- Negotiate favorable coverage with insurance companies and Pharmacy Benefit Managers (PBMs).
- Develop patient assistance programs to ensure affordability for those in need.

3. **Growth Phase**

   A. **Brand Equity Management**:

   - Monitor brand perception among HCPs and patients through surveys and market research.
   - Conduct ongoing brand awareness campaigns to maintain market share.
   - Implement loyalty programs for HCPs and patient support initiatives.

   B. **Life Cycle Management**:

   - Explore potential line extensions (new formulations, dosage strengths) to address new patient needs.
   - Conduct post-marketing surveillance to monitor the medication's safety and effectiveness.
   - Prepare for potential patent expirations and develop strategies to maintain market competitiveness.

4. **Maturity and Decline Phase**:

   A. **Competitive Landscape Analysis**:

   - Monitor the emergence of new therapies and adapt your brand positioning accordingly.
   - Consider cost-containment strategies to stay competitive in the market.

   B. **Brand Revitalization**:

   - Explore opportunities for brand refresh (new marketing campaigns, packaging updates).
   - Investigate new uses for the medication or potential repurposing for other conditions.

   C. **Exit Strategy**:

   - If the brand becomes commercially non-viable, explore licensing opportunities or potential acquisitions.

5. **Additional Prompts**:

   - How can digital marketing and social media be leveraged to reach target audiences effectively?
   - How can you use data analytics to personalize patient communication and optimize marketing efforts?

- What strategies can be implemented to ensure ongoing compliance with evolving regulations?
- How can you build strong relationships with key stakeholders (HCPs, patient advocacy groups)?

By considering these prompts throughout the lifecycle of your pharmaceutical brand, you can ensure its long-term success. Remember, the focus should be continuously innovating, adapting to market changes, and delivering value to patients and healthcare professionals.

6. Prompts for Customer Journey Mapping for Pharma Brand

1. **Understanding the Audience**:
   - Which are the different customer segments involved? (Patients, caregivers, healthcare professionals, payers).
   - What are the specific goals and needs at each stage of the journey? (**Patients**: Awareness, diagnosis, treatment options, adherence; **HCPs**: Education, treatment decisions, prescribing; **Payers**: Cost-effectiveness, access).
   - What are the common pain points and challenges faced by each segment? (**Patients**: Navigating healthcare system, managing side effects, affordability; **HCPs**: Time constraints, information overload; **Payers**: Managing costs, ensuring access).
2. **Mapping the Journey Stages**:
   - **Awareness**: How do patients and HCPs become aware of the brand and the conditions it treats?
   - **Prompts**: Marketing channels used, sources of information, initial impressions.
   - **Consideration**: How do patients and HCPs evaluate the brand compared to others?
   - **Prompts**: Research conducted, information needs, decision-making factors.
   - **Diagnosis & Treatment Decision**: How does diagnosis occur for patients, and how are treatment options presented?
   - **Prompts**: Role of HCPs, patient involvement, factors influencing treatment choice.
   - **Prescription & Access**: How do HCPs prescribe the medication, and how do patients access it?
   - **Prompts**: Insurance coverage, pharmacy interactions, patient assistance programs.

- **Treatment & Adherence**: How do patients experience the medication and manage adherence?
- **Prompts**: Side effects management, support resources, refill process
- **Outcomes & Feedback**: How do patients and HCPs evaluate the effectiveness of the treatment?
- **Prompts**: Monitoring progress, reporting side effects, patient satisfaction surveys.

3. **Additional Prompts**:
   - What touchpoints does the brand have with each customer segment at each stage? (Website, social media, doctors' appointments, patient support programs)
   - What emotional highs and lows do patients experience during their journey?
   - How can the brand personalize the customer journey for each segment?
   - What metrics can be used to measure success at each journey stage?

By considering these prompts, you can create a detailed customer journey map that will help you understand the needs and challenges of your target audience. This will allow you to develop targeted marketing strategies, Improve patient education and support, and achieve better health outcomes.

7. Prompts for Personalizing Communication for All Types of Customers (HCPs, Patients, Payers, Regulators and Investors)

1. **Understanding Your Audience**:
   - **Who are you communicating with?** (HCPs, Patients, Payers, Regulators, Investors)
   - What are their specific goals, needs, and pain points? HCPs: Time constraints, access to information; **Patients**: Understanding their condition, managing treatment; **Payers**: Cost-effectiveness, access for members; **Regulators**: Safety, efficacy data; **Investors**: Market potential, return on investment)
   - What communication channels do they prefer? **HCPs:** Email newsletters, medical conferences; **Patients**: Social media, patient portals; **Payers**: Webinars, Cost-benefit analyses; **Regulators**: Formal reports, meetings; **Investors**: Earnings calls, Investor presentations)
2. **Personalization Strategies**:
   - **Content & Language**:
     - Tailor content to their level of expertise (technical for HCPs, simpler for patients)
     - Use language relevant to their field (medical terminology for HCPs, layperson's terms for patients)
     - Highlight benefits that resonate with their goals (improved patient outcomes for HCPs, cost savings for payers)
   - **Segmentation & Targeting**:
     - Segment your audience by demographics, conditions, or other relevant factors.
     - Deliver targeted messages that address their specific needs and interests.
     - Consider offering personalized recommendations or resources (e.g., patient support programs and financial assistance options).

- **Interactive Communication**:
  - Encourage two-way communication through surveys, feedback forms, or live chat options. Address their specific questions and concerns in a personalized manner.

3. **Prompts by Customer Type**:
   - **HCPs**:
     - Highlight the medication's impact on patient outcomes and adherence rates.
     - Showcase clinical trial data and real-world evidence supporting its efficacy.
     - Offer educational resources and tools relevant to their practice area.
   - **Patients**:
     - Provide clear and concise information about the condition and treatment options.
     - Share patient testimonials and success stories for emotional connection.
     - Offer tools and resources to manage their condition and treatment (e.g., medication reminders, side effect trackers).
   - **Payers**:
     - Focus on cost-effectiveness data and potential cost savings compared to alternatives.
     - Demonstrate the medication's impact on reducing hospitalizations or readmissions.
     - Provide clear information on pricing, reimbursement, and access for patients.
   - **Regulators**:
     - Emphasize the robust clinical trial data and adherence to regulatory requirements.
     - Communicate the medication's safety profile and potential side effects.

    - Address any regulatory concerns promptly and transparently.
  - **Investors**:
    - Showcase the market potential of the medication and the target patient population.
    - Highlight the protection of intellectual property (IP) and potential for future innovation.
    - Demonstrate a clear path for commercialization and financial success.
4. **Additional Prompts**:
  - How can you leverage customer data (demographics, purchase history) to personalize communication?
  - Can you personalize the customer experience through interactive tools and self-service options?
  - How can you measure the effectiveness of your personalized communication efforts?

By considering these prompts and tailoring your message to each audience type, you can build stronger relationships with your customers, achieve your communication goals, and drive brand success.

8. Prompts for Creating a Chatbot for Patient Support

Prompt: "Susan is anxious about potential recurrence after completing her cancer treatment. Generate a chatbot script offering empathetic support, personalized resources for managing anxiety, and connecting her with other survivor communities."

Response: Chatbot Script for Susan

Introduction

Hi, Susan; thanks for reaching out. I understand you are feeling anxious about potential recurrence after completing your cancer treatment. That is completely normal, and I want you to know you are not alone.

Empathetic Support

- It is common to experience anxiety after cancer treatment. There is a lot of uncertainty, and it is okay to feel worried.
- Would you like to talk more about what is causing you anxiety?

Personalized Resources

- Here are some resources that might help manage anxiety:
- The National Cancer Institute offers relaxation techniques and information on managing cancer-related anxiety https://www.cancer.gov/clinicaltrials/NCI-2019-04134. The American Cancer Society has a program specifically designed to help people with cancer cope with fear and anxiety.
- There are also many online apps and resources available for relaxation and mindfulness, which can help manage anxiety.

Connecting with Survivor Communities

- Connecting to others who understand what you're going through can be a big help.
- There are many online and in-person support groups for cancer survivors.
- The American Cancer Society and the National Cancer Institute have resources to help you find a support group: https://www.cancer.org/support-programs-and-services.html.
- You can also search for cancer-specific support groups online or through social media.

Additional Support

- Remember, you are not alone in this. If you feel overwhelmed, don't hesitate to contact a mental health professional for additional support and guidance.
- Is there anything else I can help you with today?

Important Note

- This chatbot script is intended to provide general information and support. It is not a substitute for professional medical advice. Susan should always talk to her doctor if she has any questions or concerns about her health.

9. Prompts for Creating Healthy Lunch Options for a Diabetic Patient

Prompt: " John, a middle-aged businessman with type 2 diabetes, struggles to find healthy lunch options at work. Create a series of mobile app notifications with quick, delicious, and diabetic-friendly recipe suggestions."

Response: Diabetic Lunch Hero App Notifications for John:

Notification 1 (Monday)

Subject: **Power Up Your Work with a Salmon & Veggie Bowl!**

Hey John, conquer your Monday blues with a satisfying lunch! Grill salmon, roast broccoli, and quinoa in a salmon and veggie bowl. It's packed with protein, fiber, and healthy fats to energize you all afternoon. **Get the recipe here!**

Notification 2 (Tuesday)

Subject: Taco Tuesday with a Diabetic Twist!

Spice up your Tuesday with a Turkey Taco Salad! Ground turkey, black beans, salsa, and avocado on a bed of romaine lettuce provide a delicious and diabetic-friendly twist on a classic. The recipe is in the app!

Notification 3 (Wednesday)

Subject: Quick & Easy Wednesday Lunch! Mediterranean Wrap

Short on time? This Mediterranean Wrap is your answer! Fill a whole wheat tortilla with hummus, grilled chicken, chopped cucumber, and crumbled feta cheese for a protein and veggie-packed lunch in minutes. **Recipe details inside the app!**

Notification 4 (Thursday)

Subject: Leftover Transformation! Stuffed Butter Squash

Give leftover grilled chicken a new life with Stuffed Butter Squash! Scoop some squash and mix it with cooked chicken, chopped vegetables, and a touch of low-sugar maple syrup. Bake until tender, and enjoy a warm, comforting lunch. **Get the full recipe now**!

Notification 5 (Friday)

Subject: TGIF! Celebrate with a Shrimp Scampi with Zucchini Noodles

Treat yourself on Friday with a light and flavorful Shrimp Scampi with Zucchini Noodles!

Sauteed shrimp with garlic, lemon, and herbs served over spiralized zucchini noodles is a delicious and satisfying way to end the week. The recipe is waiting for you in the app!

Bonus Notification (Weekend)

Subject: Meal Prep for the Week Ahead!

Planning your meals can help you fight lunchtime temptations. This weekend, check out the Diabetic Lunch Hero app for delicious and healthy meal prep ideas to keep you on track throughout the week. Let's get prepped!

10. Prompts for Creating a Multi-Dimensional Value Proposition for Payers

Prompt: "You are introducing Empower, a revolutionary new drug that tackles type 2 diabetes at its core. It empowers patients and unlocks significant value for payers.

Create a compelling multi-dimensional value proposition for a payer."

Response: Empower: A Multi-Dimensional Value Proposition for Payers

Empower is not just a new drug for type 2 diabetes; It's a paradigm shift in managing the disease. Empower offers a unique opportunity to:

1. **Reduce Long-Term Costs**:
    - **Delay or prevent complications**: By effectively managing blood sugar levels at the source, Empower can help reduce the risk of costly downstream complications such as cardiovascular disease, kidney failure, and amputations.
    - **Minimize hospitalizations and readmissions:** Improved glycemic control can lead to fewer hospital stays and emergency room visits, significantly impacting healthcare spending.
    - **Decrease disease burden**: Empower's potential to slow disease progression translates into lower healthcare costs for payers in the long run.
2. **Improve Member Health Outcomes**:
    - **Enhanced quality of life**: Empower empowers patients to manage their diabetes better, improving overall health and well-being.
    - **Increased productivity**: By effectively controlling their condition, patients are less likely to miss work due to illness, which increases their productivity and economic benefits.
    - **Reduced member dissatisfaction**: By offering a revolutionary treatment option, payers can demonstrate

their commitment to providing members with the latest and most effective therapies.

3. **Administrative Efficiency:**
   - **Simplified medication management**: Empower's potential for once-daily dosing can improve medication adherence and reduce the complexity of managing multiple medications.
   - **Streamlined care coordination**: Empower's focus on addressing the root cause of type 2 diabetes can potentially streamline care coordination and reduce the need for multiple specialists.
   - **Reduced administrative burden**: Fewer complications and hospitalizations can translate to fewer administrative costs for managing complex chronic conditions.
4. **Investing in the Future**:
   - **Future-proof your population health strategy:** Empower positions payers at the forefront of innovative diabetes management, demonstrating a commitment to long-term cost savings and improved member health.
   - **Attract and retain healthy members**: By offering a revolutionary treatment option, payers can position themselves as an attractive choice for health-conscious individuals.
   - **Contribute to a healthier society**: By effectively managing type 2 diabetes, Empower can help reduce society's overall healthcare burden.

Empower is more than just a medication; it's a strategic partnership that allows payers to achieve significant cost savings, improve member health outcomes, and contribute to a healthier future. Let's unlock Empower's true value together.

Glossary

- **AI (Artificial Intelligence):** A branch of computer science concerned with creating intelligent machines capable of performing tasks typically requiring human intelligence.
- **Brand Identity:** The unique characteristics that differentiate a brand from competitors.
- **Brand Voice:** The specific tone, personality, and style a brand uses in communication.
- **Content Generation:** The process of creating new content (text, images, videos) for marketing purposes.
- **Data-Driven Insights:** Information gained from analyzing data to inform decision-making.
- **Ethical Considerations:** Concerns about the moral implications of using AI in marketing, particularly regarding bias, transparency, and data privacy.
- **HCP (Healthcare Professional):** A medical professional who provides healthcare services, such as doctors, nurses, and pharmacists.
- **Human-in-the-Loop Approach:** A collaborative approach where humans guide and oversee AI tasks, ensuring ethical and effective outcomes.
- **Iterative Refinement:** The continuous improvement through repeated testing, evaluation, and modification cycles.
- **Metrics:** Measurable data points used to track and assess the performance of marketing campaigns and content.

- **Patient Education:** Providing patients with information about their health condition and treatment options.
- **Patient Journey:** The different stages a patient goes through when diagnosed with and treated for a medical condition.
- **Pharmaceutical Marketing:** The marketing of pharmaceutical products (drugs and medications) to healthcare professionals and patients.
- **Prompt Engineering:** Crafting specific instructions and questions that guide AI models in generating desired creative text formats, like website copy, social media posts, or video scripts.

Resources for Further Learning on Prompt Engineering

Online Courses and Tutorials

- **Learn Prompting:** This website offers a comprehensive introductory course on prompt engineering, along with additional resources like papers, blog posts, and tools. https://learnprompting.org/
- **MIT Sloan Teaching & Learning Technologies:** This resource clearly explains effective prompts for AI, including best practices and limitations. https://mitsloanedtech.mit.edu/ai/basics/effective-prompts/
- **Udacity - Introduction to Artificial Intelligence Nanodegree:** This paid nanodegree program offers a broader introduction to AI, including modules on machine learning, natural language processing, and deep learning – foundational concepts for understanding prompt engineering. https://www.udacity.com/course/intro-to-artificial-intelligence/cs271

Books

- **Prompt Engineering**: The Art of Wielding Language Models by Gabriel Goldberg: This book delves into the theoretical and practical aspects of prompt engineering, providing insights into crafting effective prompts for various tasks.
- **Deep Learning with Python** by François Chollet: This book comprehensively introduces deep learning, a critical

technology underlying large language models used in prompt engineering.

Websites and Blogs:

- **Hugging Face:** This website is a hub for exploring various AI models and tools, including large language models used for prompt engineering. https://huggingface.co/
- **The Gradient by Google AI:** This blog features articles on cutting-edge advancements in AI research, including prompt engineering applications. http://research.google/blog/
- **PromptBase:** This website offers a growing collection of prompts for various creative writing tasks, inspiring prompt engineering in different domains. https://promptbase.com/

YouTube Channels:

- **Lex Fridman Podcast:** This channel features interviews with leading AI researchers, offering insightful discussions on AI technology's capabilities and limitations. https://www.youtube.com/@lexfridman
- **Yannic Kilcher** - Applied Machine Learning: This channel provides tutorials and explanations on various machine learning topics, helpful for understanding the technical aspects of AI models used in prompt engineering. https://www.youtube.com/ @YannicKilcher

Remember: The field of AI and prompt engineering is rapidly evolving. Staying updated with new resources and exploring different learning styles will ensure you stay ahead of the curve.

About the Author

Subba Rao Chaganti

He has a master's in business administration and over fifty-two years of experience in pharmaceutical marketing. His experience covers all facets of the industry, from selling to sales management, product management, and heading the total marketing activity. He has experience in domestic and international marketing and the Indian and multinational sectors.

He also taught a course on Advertising and Brand Management as an adjunct professor at Gitam Institute of Foreign Trade (now part of Gitam University) in Visakhapatnam for a few years and a course on Marketing as a visiting faculty member at Jawaharlal Nehru Technological University (JNTU) in Hyderabad.

He lives in Farmington, Connecticut, USA, and can be reached at subbarao.chaganti@gmail.com.

Here is a list of his publications:

1. Pharmaceutical Marketing in India: Concepts, Cases, Strategy
2. Game Plans for Post-Gatt Era: Action Agenda of Indian Pharmaceutical Industry
3. Compete or Forfeit: Strategies for Sustainable Competitive Advantage in Pharma Product Patents Era

4. Pharmaceutical Marketing in India for Today and Tomorrow - 25th Anniversary Edition
5. Bullseyes and Blunders: Lessons from 100 Cases in Pharma Marketing
6. Digital Pharma Marketing Playbook: Winning With the New Rules of Engagement
7. Cracking the Generics Code: Your Single-Source Success Manual for Winning in Multi-Source Product Markets
8. Reimagine Pharma Marketing: Make It Future-Proof!
9. Brand Positioning in Pharma
10. Transactional to Transformational Marketing in Pharma: The Science of Why and the Art of How!
11. A to Z of Pharmaceutical Marketing: World's First and Only Encyclopedia (Set of Two Volumes)
12. The Synergy of Minds: Human+AI Orchestrating the Pharma Marketing Revolution
13. Design Thinking for Pharma: Forget Features, Focus on Feelings
14. The Pharma Product Manager: Navigating the Digital Frontier
15. Sentiment Analysis for Pharma Marketers

www.ingramcontent.com/pod-product-compliance
Ingram Content Group UK Ltd.
Pitfield, Milton Keynes, MK11 3LW, UK
UKHW021432280726
14060UKWH00001BA/38